ESCAPE TO EXTREMADURA

A New Life in Spain's Most Remote Region

BRIAN J. WILSON

Text copyright ©2023 Brian J. Wilson

The author has asserted his moral right under the Copyright, Designs and Patents Act, 1988, to be identified as the author of this work.

All rights reserved. No part of this publication may be reproduced, stored in a retrieval system, or transmitted, in any form or by any means, without the prior permission in writing of the publisher.

1

I first met Mónica one damp Monday morning in a café on Castle Street in Clitheroe. After she'd concluded a conversation on her phone, I had the audacity to address a few words to her in Spanish, but I soon regretted my intrusion, as in the course of my brief speech I'd noticed that she seemed gloomy and preoccupied.

"Sorry, but it's so long since I heard anyone speaking Spanish," I explained in English.

The slim, olive-skinned lady smiled as she smoothed her long dark hair. "I was just talking to my brother back home," she said in clearly enunciated English. "Our father is ill and fears that he may be dying." She sighed. "I think it's time for me to go home anyway."

"I'm sorry. How long have you been in Clitheroe?"

She looked at her watch. "About two hours."

"Oh."

"But I've lived in England for almost two years." She smiled and patted the spare chair at her small corner table. "Please take a seat. I feel a need to talk to someone."

I lost no time in moving myself, my coffee, and my briefcase to her side, as it wasn't every day that an attractive forty-something lady from a country I'd always loved requested my presence. It transpired that Mónica had been an English teacher at a secondary school in Badajoz, Extremadura's principal city, until the failure of her childless marriage had led to her resigning her post and seeking a new experience as a translator and interpreter in Manchester, of all places. She was in Clitheroe purely by chance, having headed north in her car to take a walk in the Forest of Bowland, until the ominous October weather had made her opt for an urban stroll around the pretty market town instead.

"Anything to take my mind off my current dilemma. I have a trip home booked for Christmas, but no more holidays left."

"But surely if your father is... may be dying, you'll have to go."

Her brown eyes narrowed and she smiled wryly. "For my father, dying has become something of an art form in recent years. It's true that his health is poor, but he's only seventy-six and none of his ailments are life-threatening. Whenever he wishes to remind us all of his presence, he declares that the end is near. For me it's a dual dilemma, however. I'm fed up of Manchester and my tiresome job there, so I ask myself if his latest crisis might serve as a convenient excuse to resign and return home." She shrugged. "I feel a strong urge to go, but I really ought to hand in my notice and stay until Christmas."

Rather than opining on this personal matter, I complimented her on her English.

"Thank you. It's improved since I've been here. As a schoolteacher one's fluency stagnates." She smiled. "Pero ahora hablamos en castellano."

I felt my face reddening. "Oh, my Spanish is very bad. Many years ago I–"

Her raised hand stopped me in my tracks and she insisted that I attempt to express myself in that language. About thirty years earlier, after returning to my home in Kendal after a two-year spell of teaching English in Valencia, I'd initially made an effort to maintain the reasonable linguistic level I'd attained, but after my marriage I'd gradually let things slide. Despite a few short-lived attempts to knuckle down to it again, usually prior to our occasional Spanish holidays, I believed that I'd forgotten a great deal of my knowledge. While attempting to explain this to my patient listener, I realised that the long-neglected grammatical structures still lurked deep within my brain, so although I had to fill a few lexical gaps with English words, I went on to tell her that I'd divorced six years earlier and now lived in a small house in Lancaster, where I'd worked for a furniture company for twenty-odd years.

"So why are you in Clitheroe today?" she asked me in Spanish.

"I have visited a customer, on the… industrial estate."

She smiled. "Muy bien. Esto es una gran coincidencia, no?"

"Er, sí." I rubbed my balding head and grinned apologetically. "Can we speak English now, please? My brain is… tired."

"All right. Oh, we haven't even introduced ourselves."

"I'm Brian, and you are… Mónica."

She gasped. "How did you guess?"

Rather than claiming extra-sensory powers, I remarked that her brother, unlike her, had a loud voice.

"Oh, yes, Alberto does holler when he gets excited. So, Brian, here we are in a Clitheroe café. You came after seeing a customer, while I changed my plan because of the dark clouds, although it hasn't rained yet. A great coincidence, I think."

Instead of pointing out that strangers did occasionally fall into conversation even in England, I was happy to agree with her, feeling flattered by her interest in an unprepossessing middle-aged chap such as myself, merely because I'd uttered a few words in her language. When I told her that my son Ben was currently studying Spanish and French at the University of Manchester, she became convinced that fate had brought us together. I nodded and smiled, feeling glad that I'd recently had some expensive dental work carried out.

"I expect you go to visit him sometimes."

"Oh, yes," I fibbed, as after I'd driven him to his digs at the beginning of his final year, he'd hinted that further family visits would be unnecessary, as he'd shoot home on the train if he wished to see either or both of his parents.

She sipped her coffee and smiled. "Perhaps we could meet up when you next go." She frowned. "Unless I reject my brother's optimistic diagnosis and decide to go home, just in case."

Feeling ruffled and elated in equal measure, I strove to buy some time by asking her about her father's condition. She told me that besides his at least partly self-inflicted diabetes, he had a heart murmur which his doctor believed to be innocuous, high blood pressure, varicose veins, a touch of rheumatism, periodic bouts of gout, and a suspected stomach ulcer which his doctor insisted was self-inflicted indigestion.

"I see. So I take it he doesn't look after himself very well."

"He doesn't look after himself at all. He drives our poor mother to distraction, but as I say, by now we all believe that these crises are designed to make us rally round." She tutted and shook her head. "I'll call my sister Cristina later, as she's the only one of us who sees him every day."

"So are there many of you?"

She smiled. "Right now, if I'm not mistaken, the great patriarch has twenty-six descendants."

"Crikey."

"Not to mention the children he claims to have fathered during his two years of military service in Madrid." She chuckled. "His bastardos de la mili, as he calls them, though we don't believe a word of it. I'm the fourth of his eight official children. There are thirteen grandchildren, and the fifth great-grandchild was born a few weeks ago, so... yes, that makes twenty-six so far. The other day he told my brother Edu, who's the eldest, that he wished us all to gather around his bed. That isn't likely, as we're living all over the place, though mainly in Spain."

"What is he suffering from now?"

"Gout."

"Er, I don't think you can die of gout... Mónica."

"He claims that the terrible pain will cause his murmuring heart to give out, or something like that. Ah, he's such an old rogue, though I'm sure you'd like him."

Beginning to blush, I glanced at my watch. "Er, could I… would you like to have lunch at a nice pub down the street that does good food?"

She smiled. "I'd love to, Brian." She reached over and touched my cheek. "But you look a little feverish."

I believe my blush then reached an intensity not seen since childhood. "Oh, I… well, I'm not used to being so friendly with, er… attractive ladies who I've only just met."

When she laughed her white teeth seemed to sparkle.

I flattened my sparse grizzled hair, then glanced down at my flaccid belly. "Me being a bit old and not as fit as I once was."

She gazed at me earnestly. "Fate may only have brought us together as friends, Brian."

Yet more blood rushed to my beleaguered cheeks. "Oh, yes, I realise that, but I still feel pleased, you know."

"No more pleased than I do, I'm sure." She glanced down at my leather briefcase. "But don't you have work to do?"

"Oh, I often take my time over lunch," I said, my second whitish lie of the day.

In the dining room of the Swan and Royal Hotel our intimacy gradually grew, especially after I discovered that Mónica was forty-nine, a mere six years younger than me. She told me about her rather lonely life in Manchester, as she'd soon realised that most of her colleagues didn't seem to consider mixing their work and private lives the done thing, apart from a couple of tiresome married men whose dinner invitations she'd chosen not to accept. Of late she'd mainly knocked around with a Moroccan co-worker called Nadia who felt equally homesick.

"We sometimes go to classical concerts and the theatre, but as neither of us drink, we don't bother with the normal nightlife. At the weekend we often drive to the Peak District to walk in the lovely green hills."

I took a tiny sip of my half pint of bitter. "I've climbed many of the mountains in the Lake District, though not for a while."

"Ah, for Nadia and me our walks are the best thing about life here, though we spend most of the time talking about our homes. She'll return to Marrakesh in the spring to marry her long-time boyfriend, a university teacher. My contract ends in April, though I doubt I'll stay until then." She shrugged. "I'll be easy to replace, so I won't feel too guilty if I leave at Christmas, or even sooner. Tell me about your family, Brian."

This didn't take long, as both my parents had died and I saw little of my sister who lived in Devon. My son Ben no longer had much time for his boring old dad, preferring to spend most of his holidays at my spacious former home on the outskirts of Kendal.

"I'm sure your family is far more interesting than mine, Mónica."

"Hmm." She sighed and shook her head.

"What's up?"

"Oh, to me family life in England seems so... inadequate. It's as if the extended family has ceased to exist here, and for many people their home town means nothing to them, as they move away and rarely return."

"But isn't your family spread out too?"

"Ah, yes, mainly for reasons of work, but for almost all of us Llerena will always be our real home. Even my great-nephews and nieces will grow attached to the place where we've lived for many generations. Edu has spent most of his adult life in Barcelona, but a few years ago he bought a house in Llerena and will return for good when he retires."

"And the others?"

"Oh, Brian, if I start to talk about them, we'll be here until closing time." She reached over and patted my hand. "If we're to be friends, let's speak only about us for the time being. Oh, you're blushing again, you silly man. Now, tell me about this relaxed job you have which allows you to enjoy leisurely lunches with strange women."

Between nibbles of lamb chop I explained that I'd begun the job without much enthusiasm, as I'd studied economics at university and had hoped to move on to greater things, but through hard work I'd gradually made myself indispensable and had eventually become the sales manager. I told her about my swish company car, a white Tesla that I'd insisted upon having, ostensibly to compensate for all the trees that were chopped down to make our products. I then hinted that I was rather well-placed financially, despite my divorce, due to some shrewd personal investments and the fact that the value of my tidy little house had rocketed since I'd bought it.

When Mónica asked me if I intended to retire any time soon, I couldn't help but boast a little about the pension funds into which I'd been pouring most of my earnings of late, me being a frugal type with no vices to speak of.

After swallowing a morsel of plaice, she jabbed her fork at me. "It sounds to me like you're only living for the future, Brian."

I shrugged. "Oh, I don't know. I just have simple tastes, I suppose. I like reading and watching old films." I pictured the local park which I occasionally strolled around. "And like you, I'm very fond of walking."

"But you haven't answered my question."

"Which one?"

"About retirement."

The truth was that I'd been getting so much pleasure out of seeing my investments accumulate that I was reluctant to turn off the money tap any time soon. I still enjoyed my job, on the whole, and was fearful that without it I'd struggle to fill my days. Rather than confessing to this sad state of affairs, however, I was about to say that I'd pencilled in sixty as a good age to hang up my briefcase, when I found myself... not quite fibbing, but speaking in a most creative way.

"Oh, I'm not sure, Mónica. Sometimes I feel like calling it a day and beginning to live a more rewarding life. I'm in a position to do so, after all, and I have no strong ties in Lancashire any more. The weather sometimes gets me down too, so I've often thought about retiring to warmer climes. I suppose I'm just biding my time and waiting for the right moment."

She smiled. "Do you know what I think, Brian?"

"Go on."

"That you're... well, not exactly trying to impress me, but striving to say what you think I might want to hear." She sipped her water. "Sorry, now I've embarrassed you."

I rubbed my burning cheeks and sighed. "Yes, I suppose I am. I'm really an unadventurous man living a relatively pleasant life and slightly afraid of making any big changes. The owner of the company I work for is almost eighty and still comes to the office most days. He's very wealthy, but he enjoys his routine and doesn't like change. I sometimes think I'm a bit like him. When I was younger I expected to become a high-flyer in some multinational company. That's one of the reasons I decided to learn Spanish, but in the end I've been content to sell furniture in the north-west of England."

"I think most of us get what we deserve, which isn't always a bad thing. Somehow I can't picture you in a vast boardroom, smoking a big cigar."

"Me neither. I've always hated smoking, and giving orders."

Having hogged the conversation for longer than I'd intended, I asked her what she planned to do on returning home.

"Well, like you, I'm not badly off, so I expect I'll spend some time at the family home before deciding what to do. I'm loath to return to teaching, as I think twenty-two years of that is enough for me, so I might think about setting up a business."

"What kind of business?"

"I'm not sure yet. I've always felt that Llerena has potential as a tourist destination. It has such a nice square with one of the most original churches in Spain, but only one really good hotel, although it is quite marvellous. The only problem is that many towns in Extremadura have fine old buildings, so there's a lot of competition. Alternatively, some of my siblings have their fingers in various pies, as you say, so I'll go home with an open mind and see what develops."

"That sounds like the best idea."

"I am sure of one thing though. I don't want to have anything to do with pigs."

"Pigs?"

"Our famous Iberian pigs whose cured ham we export around the world."

"Ooh, yes, I'm quite partial to a bit of cured ham, though I doubt the stuff I buy in Aldi is of the best quality."

"For such a poor region I suppose it's a godsend to have something special to export, but I feel sorry for the creatures, fed mostly on acorns and destined to be slaughtered when they're fat enough. I think this is one of the reasons why I stopped eating meat a few years ago."

I pointed at the remains of her plaice. "Fish have feelings too, I suppose."

She sighed. "I know, but for fish life is a lottery which many of them win." She gazed at me. "No Iberian pig escapes the slaughterer's knife, unless they're kept for breeding, and even they normally end up having their throats cut."

"I only buy ham about once a month," I mumbled.

She laughed. "There's no need to apologise. I know it's delicious, but pigs will play no part in my business, if it happens. In the end I may lack courage and just go back to teaching, as the salary's good and I don't mind it really."

"Dessert?"

"Just coffee for me. I'd better let you get back to work soon."

I flapped my hand dismissively. "That doesn't matter. I'm my own boss, almost."

She smiled. "So when will you next visit your son in Manchester?"

I pictured Ben's face on hearing that I intended to park my Tesla outside his crummy digs in Fallowfield, before reflecting that it might be wiser to take the train if I didn't wish to find it trashed, wheel-less or absent. Besides, he wouldn't want me to cramp his style at home with his groovy housemates, so perhaps the three of us could meet up somewhere pleasant in the city centre. I smiled on realising that he'd be impressed to see me accompanied by such an attractive Spanish lady with whom he'd be able to strut his linguistic stuff…

"Brian?"

"Eh? Oh, we'll have to arrange a day that suits us all, unless you do decide to fly back to your father's bedside."

"If I do, might you come to visit me?"

Surprisingly, I didn't blush. "Yes, if you invite me."

She smiled. "I like you, Brian."

"I like you too, though I don't really know why you like me."

"Why shouldn't I like you?"

"Oh, I'm… unremarkable, and not considered especially attractive."

"Oh, who cares about that? My ex-husband looked like the famous actor Paco Rabal, in his younger days, but he was just as much of a womaniser, and no wife can be happy with a man like that. Besides, you have lovely blue eyes. They're so clear and honest."

I reddened slightly.

"And I sense that you're a very capable man."

I shrugged. "I believe I'm competent and reliable, though I've never really stepped out of my comfort zone."

She grinned. "And would you like to?"

I grinned back. "Possibly."

When the waitress brought the bill, Mónica swiftly gave her the bank card which she'd somehow secreted in her hand. When I objected, she pointed out that I'd no doubt wish to pay for our meal in Manchester, so I left a five-pound tip and escorted her outside. On the way to the car park I compared our profiles in a shop window and decided that a serious fitness campaign was long overdue. After exchanging phone numbers and email addresses by her Ford Fiesta, I suggested a WhatsApp call in a couple of days' time.

"I'd rather we just email, Brian."

"Oh, OK."

She patted my arm. "I prefer not to see or hear you again until we meet."

I raised my chin to stretch the flab beneath it. "Ah, right."

She giggled. "It may sound silly, but I want us to reflect on our encounter for a few days, before meeting again and… well, taking it from there."

I imagined Ben gawping at the pair of us. "Maybe I'll see my son first, then meet up with you later."

"Oh, no, I want to meet him. Family's very important to me." She planted two kisses firmly on my cheeks and squeezed my arm. "Hasta pronto, Brian."

"Sí, hasta pronto. Drive carefully," I said in Spanish.

"Tu también, en tu maravilloso coche eléctrico."

"Ha, yes."

After waving her off, I climbed into my marvellous electric car and called the customer in Blackburn who I couldn't be bothered to visit, having far more important things on my mind, before driving dreamily back to Lancaster through the Trough of Bowland.

Regardless of the fact that short of starving myself I'd be unlikely to lose much weight in a few days, that evening I went for a short, excruciating jog around the park, before dragging my sweaty carcass up the hill to my home and performing twenty sit-ups and fourteen press-ups, upon which my flabby arms gave out. After a refreshing shower and a tuna salad, I dug out a DVD of an amusing Pedro Almodóvar film and began to watch it with English subtitles, though I was pleased to find that I could follow much of the dialogue without them. Later, after giving my recently improved teeth a thorough flossing and brushing, I tossed the thriller I'd been reading into the corner of the bedroom and began a relatively easy Spanish novel that I'd found on my bookshelves.

After my unusually active day I soon became sleepy, so I switched off the bedside light, closed my eyes, and pictured Mónica sitting opposite me in the café and the pub. I barely had time to warn myself that surely nothing would come of our fortuitous meeting before I fell asleep.

Strange as it may sound, that night I had a hazily recalled dream in which several large pigs played a prominent part.

2

The following Saturday morning, two pounds lighter and wearing brand-new casual clothes, I punctually entered a purportedly cool Manchester café call the Koffee Pot, only to find Mónica and Ben already seated with their coffees and chatting away in Spanish.

"Hola, Papá!" my son cried as he leapt to his feet and gave me a hug. "Cómo estás?"

"Er, bien," I said, taken aback by the hug and the greeting, because we'd hardly ever spoken Spanish at home and he'd always insisted that his decision to study it had nothing to do with my long-ago sojourn in Valencia. I stepped around the slim six-footer – two inches taller than me – and kissed Mónica on the cheeks. In her stylish jacket and slacks she looked even lovelier than she had in her outdoorsy clothes, and she'd clearly made a great impression on my son during the few minutes I assumed they'd been together.

As Ben had spent half of the previous academic year in Zaragoza – prior to a few months in La Rochelle – his Spanish was fairly fluent, but after my five-day Spanish film-watching binge I was able to understand the surprising news which he took upon himself to break to me, much to Mónica's amusement.

"Is this true?" I asked her in English.

"Yes, after speaking to my sister Cristina I decided to hand in my notice at work. She fears that our father really is more poorly than usual, and certainly more tiresome, with his constant demands which are wearing out our poor mother. Cristina's busy at work, and knowing that I'm not too happy here, she's suggested that I come and take charge of the family home before the others return at Christmastime. My supervisor says that a month's notice will be sufficient, so I've already changed my flight and will leave on Saturday the 18th of November."

"Oh, I see." I managed a smile. "Are... are you pleased?"

"On the whole, yes. My future is there, so why stay here longer than I have to?"

"That's true." I turned to order a coffee, wondering where this left me in the great scheme of things.

"Llerena sounds like a great little town, Dad."

My honest blue eyes narrowed as I perused their almost empty cups. "How come you both arrived here so early?"

"I'm always early," said Ben.

"My bus arrived half an hour ago and I recognised Ben standing outside." She smiled warmly. "Another coincidence."

"Hmm, yes."

"A twist of fate," Ben said with a cheeky grin. He glanced at his phone. "I've got to be off now. I'll text you and meet up later on."

"But..."

He was on his feet. "Hasta luego, Mónica. Get my coffee, please, Dad." He smiled, saluted, and loped out of the café.

I snorted. "That's just like him."

Mónica squeezed my hand. "He's just being diplomatic, believing that we'll wish to be alone for a while."

"Oh, yes, well... so, you'll be leaving in a month then."

"Yes, but a month's a long time."

"Yes." I wondered if I'd be able to lose a stone in a month. "Yes, it's quite a long time."

She smiled. "Shall I tell you a little about my sister Cristina?" she said in Spanish.

"Sí."

Cristina was less than two years younger than Mónica and the only sibling to have spent her whole life in Llerena, having married her childhood sweetheart – a mechanic and now garage-owner called Juanjo – with whom she'd had two children who had already flown the nest. She sounded like a patient, industrious woman who had increasingly borne the brunt of the extensive preparations for the large family reunions which took place at Christmas, Easter, and in the holiday month of August, as well as many smaller incursions by brothers and sisters who managed a long weekend whenever they could.

When I asked her how on earth twenty-six people, not to mention several spouses, could be accommodated in one house, she told me that the family home was a three-storey labyrinthine sort of place which had even housed a few servants in the olden days, so they'd managed until brother Edu – short for Eduardo – had bought his house, after which they'd been able to spread out a bit. By the time we headed off for lunch she'd painted a picture of harmonious cohabitation during holiday times, when they'd all catch up with each other's news, before returning more or less contentedly to their lives in Madrid, Barcelona, Badajoz, Cáceres, Salamanca and Monchengladbach, where the youngest brother, Alejandro, worked as a mechanical engineer.

"It sounds like bedlam to me," I said in English as we took our seats in the quiet Italian restaurant.

"Bedlam? Oh, you mean very noisy? Well, it can be at times, but once I've bought my house, we'll have even more space in which to relax at those busy times of year."

"So are you going to buy a place in Llerena?"

She smiled. "Yes, I think so. I've been thinking about it during the last few days and it makes a lot of sense. In Llerena and the nearby villages there are plenty of cheap properties at the moment. For as little as €40,000 one can buy a modest house or flat in need of reform, and for twice that amount there are many better options. I believe prices can only rise, so it'll be a good investment, and also good for me psychologically."

"Why's that?"

"Oh, I've always known that I'd wish to return to my roots one day. I mean, why live elsewhere when one's home town is pleasant, familiar and affordable? I'll be fifty next year and I feel the need for a little stability. Whatever I decide to do, a house is always an asset, even if I don't live in it just yet. Are you going to have a pizza?"

"Yes, I think so."

"Then I'll have one too. So, Brian, when are you going to visit me?"

"Oh, well, I could come out any time, but preferably not at Christmas."

She laughed. "Oh, my family narrative has frightened you."

"Just a bit. When I was a boy I seem to remember there being up to ten people in our house at Christmas, but that diminished over the years." I elected not to admit that I'd spent the previous Christmas Day alone. "I'll come at a quiet time, if that's all right."

"Of course, though we have plenty of time to get to know each other before I leave."

I smiled. "That's true." I considered inviting her up to Lancaster, but thought it might sound a bit forward. "I'm always free at the weekends."

"Good, then you'll be able to stay at my flat tonight."

I gulped and began to blush. "I... I didn't bring a toothbrush."

She tittered. "I believe they sell them in Manchester."

"Hmm, yes."

"I have a sofa-bed, should you wish to use it."

"I... I don't know what to say, Mónica."

"Then don't say anything. The vegetarian pizza sounds good. I think I'll have that."

I eschewed my usual pepperoni and ordered the same.

Over our meal she quizzed me about my current life and I found myself admitting to its inadequacies more readily than I had during our first meeting, partly because in the intervening days I'd realised that my lifestyle left a lot to be desired. Apart from popping into the local pub once or twice a week, I spent most of my free time alone. I had to be quite sociable at work, in order to keep the sales coming in, so it was only at the weekends when it occasionally dawned on me that I'd begun to resign myself to bachelorhood. After conveying this to Mónica in a light-hearted sort of way, she opined that I was too young to be living such a hermetic life, and if I wasn't careful I'd find myself in a rut that I'd never get out of.

"So do you think I'm in a rut?"

She shrugged. "That depends really. I mean, would you say that you're living a life of the mind?"

I pictured the discarded thriller which I'd since binned. "Well, I do read good books and watch thought-provoking films, but I read and watch a lot of rubbish too, so the answer is no, not really. I guess I just chug along, waiting for something to happen."

She smiled. "And has it?"

I pushed away my plate, having left most of the fattening crusts. "Can I be frank with you, Mónica?"

"That's exactly what I want you to be."

"Well, it's like this." I cleared my throat. "The other day I was delighted to meet you and I've been thinking about you ever since." I plucked at my designer sweatshirt. "These clothes are new and I've been working out every day, as well as studying Spanish. I felt a great sense of anticipation all the way here in the train and my... my heart leapt when I saw you sitting there with Ben." I sipped my ginger beer. "Then, when you said you were going home... well, I feared that I'd been getting my hopes up too much."

She smiled. "I suppose you'd have liked me to stay here for a few more months."

"Well, I guess that would have suited me better, but I think you're right to go."

"If you wished to, would you be able to get a sabbatical from work?"

I gasped. "A sabbatical?"

"Yes. Can't you ask your boss for two or three months off? You could tell him you're having a mid-life crisis or something."

I couldn't help but laugh. "Oh, Mónica, old George, my boss, probably doesn't even know what a sabbatical is, and as for a mid-life crisis, well, he'd just tell me not to be so bloody soft. He's very old-school is George, bless him. He looks after his workers, but he believes they should be as keen as him. He's mentioned making me a partner before long, as he doesn't trust his son to go on with the business alone after he's gone, so I'm afraid a sabbatical is out of the question." I smiled and patted her hand. "Much as I'd like to have one."

To this day I still wonder if Ben had been hiding behind one of the wicker partitions, because at this precise moment he bore down on our table and flopped into the spare chair.

"Women," he uttered on exhaling in an apparently breathless manner.

"What about us?" Mónica enquired.

"Oh, I've just had a burger with this bir… girl from the faculty who I like, but I can't make head nor tail of her. She'll meet me during the day but says she doesn't want us to get too close in case I take advantage of her. I mean, can you believe that, in this day and age?"

"Yes, I can," I said primly.

"Yeah, well, you're like an old monk or something, festering away in that titchy house of yours."

"Excuse me," said Mónica, before making for the bathroom.

"Right, where are you up to?" Ben murmured.

"In what respect?"

"Are you going to chuck that boring job of yours and stroll off into the sunset with that lovely lady?"

I sighed. "Ben, Mónica isn't some bird from the faculty, and I'm not a footloose student like you. We've only just met, so I certainly won't be making any snap decisions on the basis of my… infatuation."

He leant back in his chair and tugged at his wavy locks. "Oh, lordy, you're even more of a fuddy-duddy than I thought you were."

"I admire your sincerity."

He suddenly thrust himself forward, grasped my wrists, and eyeballed me from close quarters. "Don't be a chump, Dad. You've got to strike while the iron's hot."

I recalled Mónica's overnight invitation. "Yes, well, I'm sure we'll get to know each other better in due course. She isn't leaving for a month, after all. Can you let me go now?"

He released my wrists and prodded the end of my stubby nose with his index finger. "Mónica's just what you need, Dad. I was hoping that something would happen to drag you out of this rut you're in, but I never imagined you'd get so lucky. I haven't a clue what she sees in you, but she seems to think you're a really wonderful guy. If I met someone like her – of my age, I mean – I'd go to the ends of the earth with her, no matter what."

"How romantic."

"Yeah, well, you know what'll happen if you're not careful, don't you?"

"Please enlighten me."

"She'll go home and you'll arrange to visit her when that old bastard gives you a week off, right?"

"Old George isn't a ba–"

"Shush. But what I think you're too dense to realise is that as soon as she lands back in her home town, every eligible bloke of a certain age is going to be following her round with his tongue hanging out."

I smiled placidly. "Let them. That sort of test is no bad thing, anyway."

"Yeah, unless some old childhood sweetheart who's got tons of money and has just got divorced or something steps in and woos her while you're flogging bloody furniture in some dismal dump. All's fair in love and war, remember, and being back home might make her see things differently."

I suddenly recalled a lovely girl called Chloe who I'd known as a student in Liverpool. We became quite close, but due to the spectre of a supposed boyfriend back home I failed to declare my feelings for her, thinking it more gentlemanly to wait until she'd broken up with him. In the meantime, a soon-to-be ex-pal of mine stepped into the breach and whisked her off her feet. They went on to marry and as far as I knew were still living happily ever after…

"Dad?"

"Eh? Oh, yes, I see what you mean. I shall bear your wise words in mind, Ben."

To this day I still wonder if Mónica had been biding her time behind that same wicker partition, because she now strode nonchalantly back to the table and suggested that we order coffee.

"I must dash," said Ben as he rose to his feet. "I've got a band practice."

"Where's your guitar?"

He grinned. "In my mate's car."

Mónica stood up. "It's been lovely to meet you, Ben." They exchanged kisses. "Will I see you tomorrow before your dad leaves?"

"Maybe. Enjoy yourselves." He loped out.

"What a charming son you've got, Brian."

"Yes, he's a peach."

"And he speaks pretty good Spanish too. I'm sure he'd be a hit with the girls in Llerena."

"Ha, yes, we could both come to live in your house, when you get it."

"Ben has to finish his degree, and I doubt there'd be any rewarding work for him to do in my out of the way little town."

"Yes, well, I was joking, really."

"You, on the other hand, wouldn't necessarily have to do any work, although I doubt a man of your age and temperament would wish to idle away his days."

"Er, well, I… I…"

She chuckled. "Don't worry, Brian. I'm a realist at heart, but it can do no harm to think ahead a little, can it?"

"Not at all."

Shall I tell you about my brother Alejandro, who lives in Germany?" she said in Spanish.

"Sí. Por qué está viviendo allí?"

"Well, his company wanted him to spend just two years in Monchengladbach, but after he met Irma, now his wife, he insisted on staying. His bosses wouldn't allow this, so he improved his German and found a job with a smaller company there. At first he earned less money, but now he's doing well. They have a son called Kasper who'll be eleven now, but we haven't seen them since last Christmas. Alejandro's the only one of us who has really flown the nest for good, I think. Kasper speaks very little Spanish, which is a shame, but he and Alejandro have become part of Irma's family, so I suppose he's a true emigrant, unlike me, as I've never ceased to miss my home."

"A true love story too, I suppose, risking his career in order to stay with her."

She smiled. "He knew she was the one for him from the moment they met. You look pensive, Brian."

"Hmm, do you remember telling me that you had no holidays left."

"Yes, though that doesn't matter now."

"The next day at the office I asked about mine. It turns out I've accumulated seven weeks, as I didn't take them all last year or the year before."

"Oh, was there nowhere you wanted to go?"

I shrugged. "I guess not. It's just struck me that all seven weeks in a row would make a sort of sabbatical."

Although Mónica looked pleased, I sensed that she didn't wish to make any bold suggestions just yet.

Perhaps she wants to be sure that the physical side of our relationship goes smoothly, I thought as she took my hand outside the restaurant, but after shopping romantically for a toothbrush I felt sure that it would, despite my lengthy sabbatical from sex.

"Do we need to buy anything else?" I asked her as we strolled contentedly along Market Street.

"No, at the flat I have everything we need." She patted the little parcel in my jacket pocket. "I even bought you a toothbrush, but when you mentioned it I didn't wish to seem too forward."

Then, with fearless gallantry, I drew her to me and kissed her lightly on the lips.

"Oh, Brian."

"Ah, Mónica."

Presently, on reaching High Street, a taxi slowed to a halt on seeing my raised hand, a minor miracle and a splendid omen if ever I saw one.

"Oh, Brian, how assertive of you."

"I know, I know."

3

On awakening to the smell of fresh coffee tickling my nostrils, it dawned on me that I hadn't been brought a cuppa in bed for almost thirty years, since the very early days of my marriage. That morning we mostly lazed around, and I believe there was no doubt in either of our minds that our relationship had taken a gigantic step forward. Since my marriage had ended I'd positively enjoyed sleeping alone, apart from a short-lived affair three years earlier, but I knew that my solitude would no longer feel so sweet.

When we finally made an effort to rise at about eleven, Mónica told me she had a confession to make.

"Oh, I'd rather not hear about any lovers you've had."

She tittered. "Only one little fling during four years as a single woman, but it's not that. Look at this." She parted the hair on the crown of her head.

I searched for dandruff but couldn't see any. "What?"

"Can't you see bits of grey? I dye my hair, you see."

"Oh, my God," I wailed histrionically. "Why didn't you tell me? I'd never have stayed if I'd known."

"Cheeky devil. It's only slightly grey and I'd like to stop dying it really."

I ran my hand through her glossy locks. "You do that if you wish, love. Then you won't look so much younger than me."

"You don't seem old to me. You have a certain naivety that I like very much."

"Yes, and my fitness campaign is well under way." I slapped my belly. "This will soon be gone." As she dressed I admired her strong legs and slender body. "What do you do to keep fit?"

"Only walking. I'll miss the Peak District, and my friend Nadia, but back home, to the south of Llerena, there are lots of tracks and paths through the woods where we'll be able to walk for miles."

"Will we see vultures?" I said, having already begun to do a little research into the area.

"I believe there are some there, though when I was young I didn't see the attraction of the countryside. My friends and I preferred to catch the bus or train to Zafra, about half an hour away. It seemed like a city to us small town girls. Ah, the space and quiet of Extremadura will be a great relief after two years in this crowded country. Even in the Peaks we'd often find large numbers of people heading for the same summit."

"But no vultures."

"No, though we did see an eagle once."

The subject of vultures brought to mind my employer. Although George was a benevolent old bird, on the whole, if he spotted any carrion in the firm – by which I mean slackers – he'd soon eat them up and spit them out, so I wasn't sure how he'd react when I requested a seven-week holiday. Under normal circumstances I'd have eventually accepted payment for most of those weeks, but my life had changed overnight and I felt a strong urge to fly away with Mónica in a month's time and stay with her until the new year. That way I'd be with her right from the start and would still be there when the whole family descended on Llerena at Christmastime. I imagined that out relationship would have blossomed by then and I would only return to Lancaster to prepare my successor at work and sort out my affairs, before returning to Spain for good…

"A penny for your thoughts, Brian."

I put this plan of action to her and by way of reply she pinned me to the bed and squeezed the air from my lungs.

"Old George won't like it," I said when I'd got my breath back.

"Old George has his life and you have yours. He must respect your wishes."

"Hmm." I tapped the bedpost.

Later on, Mónica drove us to Fallowfield and we paid Ben an impromptu visit in his student hovel.

"Is there anywhere safe to eat around here?" I asked him after declining his invitation to sit on the foul-looking sofa.

"Course there is. Wilmslow Road's full of great cafes. You look a bit stressed, Mónica."

"Oh, I think my shoes have stuck to the carpet."

"Yeah, it happens. I'll be ready in five. Make yourselves at home."

"We'll guard the car."

"Fallowfield's fine nowadays. You ain't half led a sheltered life, Dad."

"Yes, well, I have some news for you, so get a move on."

In the cosy Turkish café, where smoking shisha pipes had only recently been banned by Manchester's reactionary council, we ate sandwiches and sipped the delicious coffee. On hearing my news, Ben unnerved me somewhat by considering my forthcoming holiday request a fait accompli.

"Er, you only met old George once, and he's always nice to visitors. He might be a tough nut to crack."

Ben wagged a finger at me. "You can't let that grasping old fart spoil your plans, Dad. You've got to *tell* him you're taking the time off. Then, once you've been there for a while and everything's hunky-dory, you phone him and resign. End of story." He gazed at us and grinned. "Because I can tell that you've got off to a flying start, eh?"

I blushed.

Mónica squeezed my hand and smiled at Ben. "Those seven weeks would be ideal, but not essential. I believe we both know what we want to do, but there's no great hurry to commence our life together. One must act responsibly, after all."

Ben eyeballed me. "I'll call you tomorrow evening. If you chicken out, I'll be giving you a bollocking that you won't forget in a hurry."

"Yes, son."

When he asked Mónica what the young ladies of Llerena were like, she told him to come out at Christmas and find out for himself.

"I sure will. How do you get there?"

"Malaga and Faro airports are a little nearer than Madrid, but they're all quite distant. Madrid is usually the best option. From Barajas airport you take the metro to Atocha station and a train to Cáceres, then a train or a bus to Zafra, where we'll pick you up. One can usually arrive home from the airport in six or seven hours."

"Wow, it sounds like the Wild West."

"It is in a way. Extremadura has always been the most isolated region of Spain. I sometimes think our famous conquistadors went off to discover new lands out of sheer boredom, although they usually came back to build great churches and other monuments to themselves."

"I've been doing some research," I said. "But I think I'll stop now, or I'll end up going with too many preconceived ideas. I'll just concentrate on improving my Spanish." I sucked in my belly. "And getting fit."

Ben shook his head and sighed contentedly. "This seems too good to be true."

"I know. I can't believe my luck."

"Me neither," said Mónica.

I puffed out my chest. "Tomorrow I'll tell old George what's what."

"You *what*?" old George bellowed across the desk of his scruffy old office.

I smile weakly. "You heard, George."

Not yet being au fait with internet banking, although his office staff were, he pulled a chequebook from a drawer. "I'll pay you for four of those weeks right away. The other three will be plenty between now and Easter. By all mean trot off for a week with this new lass of yours, but you know how busy we get coming up to Christmas."

"Denise and Mike can easily cover for me."

He slapped the desk with his gnarled, office-hardened hand. "But you're the man who has to get new customers. With this bloody Ikea and whatnot we can't rest on our laurels." He stared at me so fiercely that I began to fear for his sanity. "I *need* you to keep the business coming in." He flashed his implants in what was meant to be a conniving smile. "And it'll soon be time to give you a stake in the company. How does a quarter share sound? Just think of the money you might make, once we've paid for those new machines. I'm still on the ball, but I'm not getting any younger, and I can't trust my Chris to sail this ship alone."

"Give me a minute to think, George."

When he began to light his noisome pipe, sucking and puffing like some kind of Dickens' character, his mention of new customers reminded me of the innumerable contacts I had in the furniture trade. Should the honeymoon period which Mónica and I had begun not develop into a long-lasting relationship, I'd have no difficulty in finding another job, albeit on a smaller salary and without my silky-smooth Tesla. Reassured by this, I elected to be completely honest with my boss and told him that my seven-week sabbatical would probably be the beginning of the end of my long career at the firm, as I wished to start a new life in Spain.

He glared at me through a smoky haze. "Where did this bloody woman pop up from anyway?"

"I've been seeing her for... some time. We're in love and wish to make a life together."

He shook his bald head sadly. "I never saw you as one of these lazy sods who retire at fifty-five. Have you no *ambition* left?"

"Yes, but not here." I pushed my chair back, to stay out of the carcinogenic cloud and also to avoid any missiles which might be heading my way, but poor old George just tossed his pipe onto the desk and flopped back in his ancient swivel chair.

"Do what you like," he muttered. "I'm getting sick of the sight of this place anyway. Nearly sixty bloody years of work, and what do I have to show for it?"

A splendid house on the edge of Lake Windermere that you hardly ever go to, I thought.

"Look, I'll do all I can to make sure everything runs smoothly after I've gone. Why don't you, er... sort of follow my lead and begin to hand over the reins to... others?" I said hopefully, though at seventy-nine he was getting a bit old to start using the golf clubs we'd gifted him almost twenty years earlier.

He sat up straighter and smiled. "That's very thoughtful of you, Brian."

I shrugged. "It's an idea."

He pushed himself to his feet and began to drum his fingers ominously on the edge of the desk while looking directly over my head. I tensed my thighs, ready to bolt for the door, but he didn't pick up the paperweight which he claimed to have hurled at a shop steward back in the seventies.

"Now piss off out of here, Brian, and start handing over *your* reins right away."

I stood up. "Will do. Can I take on someone new, if I think that's the best way forward?"

He turned to face the grimy window overlooking another factory unit. "Aye, go ahead. I'll tell you one thing though. Spain isn't all it's cracked up to be. Folk are coming back in droves, and once this Brexit thing finally happens the rest of the lazy buggers might get chucked out too. Where will you be then, young fellow-me-lad?"

In the bosom of a large Spanish family, I hoped.

"Well, I can always come crawling back and ask you for a job," I said.

He turned to face me. "Aye, and I'd probably give you one too." He wagged a finger at me. "But don't forget that women are fickle creatures, nice as pie one minute and nagging like mad the next. I know you haven't been seeing this one for long, because I saw you'd changed last week." He sighed. "I thought you might have come up with a great new customer, but it turns out you've found yourself a new ball and chain. Anyway, get to work and do as you see fit."

"I suppose I'd better write you a letter of resignation."

"If you like. I'll leave it in my drawer, in case you change your mind." He turned back to the window. "I trust you to do right by me, after so long together."

"I will. Thanks, George."

"Hmm."

After leaving him staring glumly at the cloudy sky, I tried to quell my feeling of elation and concentrate on the task at hand, because once I'd flown away with Mónica I didn't want to return to work if I could possibly help it.

Rather than dedicating a chapter to the hectic month which followed, punctuated by delightful weekends with Mónica, mostly in Lancaster, I'll cut to the chase and move on to the main theme of this account, save to say that during that time I was able to set the ship I was abandoning on an even keel, I believed, and thus end my career in a satisfying way. George was enough of a gent to give me a handsome final bonus, and in return I agreed to act as an unpaid consultant for a while – as the wily old fox probably guessed I would – but only at a distance of about 1,500 miles.

I decided to rent out my house through an agency, thus enabling me to store many of my possessions in the loft. Due to its furnished state, they soon received a few enquiries from temporary university lecturers and the like, as after seeing Ben's hovel I'd told them I wanted no students turning it into a sticky-floored war zone. My son had in fact convinced me to rent rather than sell. Although he thoroughly approved of Mónica, he insisted that he had far more experience with women than I did, and that until we'd lived together for at least a year we wouldn't be sure if we were really made for each other.

I frowned at the screen through which he was dispensing this wise advice.

"What's up, Dad?"

"Oh, I was just wondering what it'll be like at her parents' house."

"Quite an experience, I bet. In at the deep end, eh?"

I gulped. "Sí."

4

It felt good to be back on Spanish soil for the first time in over a decade, and even better when we'd put the irksome part of our journey behind us and were seated on the comfortable, half-empty train to Cáceres. Once we'd left the huge Madrid conurbation I feasted my eyes on the sun-drenched plains which I hadn't seen since my time in Valencia, as in the intervening years all my visits had been to the coast. Beyond Talavera de la Reina we glimpsed the Sierra de Gredos a long way to the north and a similarly distant mountain range to the south. I marvelled at the vastness of it all.

"Yes, I'm already breathing more easily," Mónica said from the window seat opposite mine. "One has to go away to truly appreciate what we have in this part of Spain from which people have been forced to flee for many decades, always in search of work."

"Yes, it's a shame they couldn't… diversify or something."

She pointed at a massive tractor ploughing the land. "That thing does the work of fifty men. They need very few human hands to harvest cereals. Many of my parents' generation emigrated, to Germany, France, even the Americas, but those who could usually returned." She chuckled. "Like little modern conquistadors, coming home with their riches."

I sighed. "I'm going to miss speaking English with you, if you're serious about what you said."

She smiled. "Yes, once we reach Cáceres we switch to Spanish. That's the best way for you to become fluent quickly."

"Speaking Spanish tires my brain."

"That's because you're constantly translating from English. From now on you must speak Spanish or be silent. In a few weeks it'll become second nature to you. Ah, any time now we'll be in Extremadura. Look, we're already entering an area of dehesa."

I gazed at the small, irregularly spaced trees – mostly holm and cork oaks – on the flattish grassland which was only good for grazing.

"You seem fascinated by it, Brian."

"I'm hoping to spot my first Iberian pig. I've never been west of Toledo before."

"Ah, did you enjoy visiting that wonderful city?"

"Hmm, I mainly remember the terrible hangover I had after we'd spent an evening carousing in the taverns, but I was young and foolish then. Ooh, look, a big fat black pig. It looks like it's snuffling for truffles or something."

"Probably acorns," she said glumly.

"Oh, sorry, I forgot that you're not keen on pigs."

"It's their fate I'm not keen on."

I gazed at the dehesa stretching away into the distance. "So is that all this land's good for, fattening pigs?"

"They also harvest the cork every decade or so, and there's a lot of hunting at certain times of year."

"Oh, do they go out and shoot the poor pigs?"

"I believe a few idle aristocrats used to do that, but there are also wild boars which are considered fair game. Most hunters settle for rabbits, hares, partridges and other birds, and deer where there are any. Foxes too… anything that moves, really."

"I take it from your expression that we won't be setting up a hunting business any time soon."

"No, Brian, we won't be doing that."

A while later she pointed out something glittering away to the north. "Many believe that our future prosperity will rely on things like that."

"Oh, yes, solar panels, and we've already seen plenty of wind turbines."

Mónica then told me that Extremadura was said to be generating all of its energy from renewable sources and had begun to sell the surplus to the rest of Spain. As well as solar and wind power, they were producing a lot of biomass energy whose environmental credentials were a hot topic of debate, as burning the plant matter inevitably contaminated the atmosphere.

"Maybe we should put some solar panels on the roof of our house," I said, as we'd already spoken about purchasing a property together, though not just yet, in case our relationship failed to prosper. I was so besotted with Mónica that I couldn't imagine tiring of her, but I did fear that she might fall out of love with me if I didn't get along with her folks. I intended to try my best, of course, though I'd already hinted that renting a place not far from the family home could be our best bet in the short to medium term. She'd agreed that this might be a sensible option, though she seemed more concerned about what we'd do rather than where we'd live.

She now raised this subject once again by asking me what I really thought of rural tourism.

"I'm all for it."

She rubbed my left ankle with her right foot and asked me if I thought British people would be interested in such a peaceful but far-flung place as a holiday destination.

"Er, I haven't seen it yet."

She pointed at the cereal fields we were then hurtling past. "To the north and east of town it's much like this. To the west there are many fields of olive and almond trees, and to the south we have miles and miles of wild dehesa and some real woodland, but far hillier than here. Ah, it's so quiet and isolated that it makes the Peak District seem like some kind of holiday park." Her brown eyes narrowed. "I have a hunch that our destiny lies somewhere to the south, though I don't really know why."

"Are there many houses there?"

"Hardly any."

"Well then?"

She shrugged. "It's only a hunch. There is of course the... oh, have you done any more research recently?"

"No, I've been strong and haven't been googling anything about the area. I want you to show it to me."

"I will, and there's one special attraction not far from Llerena that you'd have mentioned if you'd found out about it."

"What's that?"

She grinned. "You'll soon see."

In Cáceres we had over an hour to kill, so we bundled our three suitcases and two large rucksacks into a taxi and Mónica asked the driver if he'd mind becoming our tour guide for a while.

The friendly young chap smiled. "While the meter is ticking, we can do whatever you wish."

Thus it was that we did a whistle-stop tour of the historic city centre. The immense, almost traffic-free Plaza Mayor took my breath away, and while our driver guarded our belongings we walked up to the really old part of town – a Unesco World Heritage Site – where renaissance churches and palaces abounded but few tourists were to be seen, despite some filming for Game of Thrones having recently taken place there.

"I'm surprised it isn't chock-a-block with sightseers on such a sunny Saturday afternoon."

"Perdón?"

"I'm surprised… oh, gawd, is it time to speak Spanish?"

She squeezed my hand. "Sí."

I repeated my statement in simple Spanish, and from now on, unless I state otherwise, every conversation I attempt to reproduce will be translated from my adopted language, though I'll spare you my many mistakes unless they prove amusing in any way. This new regime made for a peaceful half hour, as I lacked the descriptive vocabulary necessary to wax lyrical about the splendid buildings. As we made our way down a cobbled street to the square I explained the reason for my taciturnity.

"That's all right. It's nice to be quiet sometimes and just soak up the atmosphere."

"Sí."

In the taxi the driver asked Mónica why the foreign gentleman had ceased to talk.

"He's been rendered speechless by the beauty of old Cáceres."

"Sí," I concurred.

He grinned at me in the rear-view mirror. "Ah, so you understand Castilian?"

"Er, sí."

All the way to the bus station he spoke rapidly into the mirror and waved his arms around to illustrate the more salient points of his discourse.

"...don't you think?" I caught as he applied the handbrake.

"Sí."

"Have a good trip."

"Gracias."

When the half-empty coach reached the almost deserted southbound dual carriageway, Mónica asked me if I was angry about something.

"Angry, no, just… disappointed, and a little worried."

"Por qué?"

"I understand your Spanish very well, and quite a lot in the films I have watched, but that taxi driver, almost nothing."

"Ah, sí, the Cacereños do speak very quickly and not very clearly."

"And the Lleren... Llerena people?"

"The Llerenenses speak a little more slowly, on the whole."

"And more clearly?"

"Well, not really, but you'll soon get used to it."

"Oh, my God. Your family will think I am deaf, dumb and stupid."

She giggled. "Of course they won't. I've already told them you're an intelligent man."

"So how is it that I understand you so well, Mónica?"

She explained that being a language teacher enabled her to gauge the linguistic ability of whoever she addressed and adjust the pace and content of her speech accordingly.

"With you, for instance, these last few weeks when we've spoken Castilian I've been gradually increasing the complexity of my diction and speaking more quickly."

"Ah, vale," I said, meaning OK, a word I could see myself using an awful lot. "I understand Fernando Rey really well," I added, referring to one of the greatest Spanish actors, several of whose films I'd recently enjoyed.

"Yes, he was wonderful. What about other Spanish actors and actresses? Did you understand them?"

"Sometimes, but sometimes I... excuse these English words, I let it wash over me and just got the gist."

"Hmm, sí, that's partly because you knew you wouldn't need to reply. I suggest you do the same in Llerena, especially with my father. That's what the rest of us normally do."

"Vale. In a while we will enter Mérida. I believe there are many Roman… things there."

"Roman remains, sí. Do you like them?"

"Sí."

"Muy bien. We'll come to spend the weekend when we feel the need for a rest."

"And when do you think that will be?"

"Probably next weekend."

After trundling into the town centre to drop a lot of people off, the quarter-full coach headed south on a bypass.

"Look, Brian, along the river you can see the Roman bridge."

"Ooh, sí. How impressive. I don't suppose the Romans got as far as Llerena."

She turned away to look upriver. "Not quite. Let's try to sleep for half an hour. Then you'll be fresh when we reach Zafra."

I yawned and closed my eyes. "Vale."

5

Because Cristina had spent her whole life in Llerena and married a motor mechanic, I'd expected her to be more homely than Mónica – not having been naturally selected away into the world, so to speak – but she was even more beautiful than my sweetheart, her smooth olive skin belying her forty-seven years. Her cheerful expression suggested that her father's gradual recovery from his latest near-death experience had taken a weight from her mind, and after I'd been introduced and pecked firmly on each cheek, I enquired about his health.

"Much better, gracias. His gout has almost gone and he's now able to move around the house, harassing our poor mother."

"Ah, that's good."

Mónica explained that my wide smile and upbeat reply to this mixed news was probably due to the fact that I'd understood her, unlike the gabbling taxi driver in Cáceres.

Cristina smoothed back her long dark hair and raised her chin slightly. "Ours is an old, respected family, Brian. We don't speak like the humble folk."

"Vale."

Her brown eyes sparkled mischievously. "I'm joking, a little."

"Ah."

"Though some snobbishness still prevails in our family," said Mónica. "As you will see."

Cristina glanced at the nearby bus station toilets and sniffed. "Let's get out of here."

There wasn't time to show me the sights of Zafra, but as Llerena was only forty kilometres away Mónica told me we'd have plenty of opportunities to explore its old buildings, including a fifteenth century castle.

"Wow," I said fluently.

"But Llerena is far more interesting," Cristina said as she clicked open the doors of an old but impeccably preserved silver Mercedes saloon.

"I'm looking forward to seeing it."

I'd pinpointed Llerena on the map, of course, and as we bowled along a flat, almost deserted main road I assumed it would be something of a backwater. Zafra itself was a town of only sixteen thousand inhabitants, though it was quite well communicated, but Llerena seemed to be slap bang in the middle of nowhere. Seville lay about eighty miles to the south, on the other side of the verdant Sierra Morena, with Cordoba a little further to the south-east, but to the east and north-east there were nothing but villages and the odd small town until one reached Ciudad Real, about 150 miles away. To the west there were few settlements of any great size before the border with Portugal, and even the provincial capital, Badajoz, was an hour and a half's drive away to the north-west. So, as Llerena was home to fewer than 6,000 souls, I made ready to enthuse about the big old church surrounded by a huddle of houses which I fully expected to see.

On the mostly straight road between the vast cereal fields I pondered on the hundreds of people who would have worked that land in the olden days and realised how the mechanisation of agriculture must indeed have sent many of them packing to the cities or abroad. I recalled how as a teenager I'd helped to load bales of hay onto a trailer at my friend's uncle's farm near Kendal, but the great cylindrical bales I saw dotted around could only be lifted by machines.

Mónica turned to smile at me. "Look, now we can see the hills to the south."

I gazed at the hazy wooded undulations. "Ah, sí."

"Almost there now."

"Muy bien." Still, I mused, what did living in a one-horse town in the middle of the dusty plains matter, as long as I was with my own true love? It was only natural that she saw the place through rose-tinted specs, after all, and no matter how dull and backward it proved to be, I was determined to conceal the disappointment I was bound to feel.

"That is the biggest supermarket," Cristina said as we approached a grassy roundabout containing a quaint structure with a couple of old millstones. "And the little hospital is just over there."

"Our father is one of their regular customers," said Mónica.

As we drove along a wide street with a series of palm trees on one side and white three-storey buildings on the other, it reminded me of places I'd visited near the coast. Our route into the centre was thoroughly modern, in fact, and none of the folk strolling around in the fading light were dressed in black or chewing straw. Functional was the word which sprang to mind as we passed neat rows of houses interspersed with small green spaces, but at least it seemed civilised and probably had good internet connections, judging by the number of youngsters I saw goggling at their phones.

"We're driving around the centre to our house now," said Cristina.

"Ah, bien."

"Shall we show him the Plaza de España?" Mónica asked her.

"Hmm, do you think he'll want to see it?"

"Well, he might as well have a look at our humble square."

As she turned onto a narrow street of older houses, Cristina feigned a yawn. "All right, but don't get too excited, Brian."

"I will try not to."

"One cannot expect too much from such an isolated little town."

"No."

"Many kilometres from the centres of civilisation," said M.

"Hmm."

"An insignificant place which few people know about."

"Ah."

Cristina pulled into one of the many free parking spaces. "Here we are."

"Bloody hell! Oh, perdón. Er… santo cielo," I said, meaning good heavens. "This… this is like the square in Cáceres, only smaller."

Cristina tittered. "We like it."

"And we enjoy showing it to people for the first time."

"It is a beautiful square, and what a marvellous church. It is unexpected, after… the rest."

"The rest of our boring town, you mean?" said Mónica. "Well, this church is by no means the only significant building we have, as you'll see, but I do recall telling you that it's one of the most original in Spain."

I gazed up at the tall, ornate tower, but it was a double row of white arches stretching along the side of the building, above what appeared to be the main entrance, which impressed me most. Once we'd climbed out of the car, I asked them what the arches were for.

"Oh, they're an eighteenth-century addition, built so that the town's dignitaries could observe what was going on in the square," said Mónica. "Bullfighting used to take place here, as well as markets and festivities. Have you heard of the painter Francisco de Zurbarán?"

"Ah, sí, I saw some of his pictures in the Prado museum." I smiled proudly at Cristina. "A long time ago."

"He was born in a nearby village and lived in a house in this square for about fifteen years," she said, seeming impressed by my lofty cultural level, although it was Zurbarán's name rather than his paintings which had stuck in my mind for so long, as I recall whizzing around the Prado like a man possessed in my quest to see it all before catching the train back to Valencia.

"He was a great renaissance master," I assured her.

"Yes, he was known as the Spanish Caravaggio, although here we like to say that Caravaggio was the Italian Zurbarán."

"Even though Caravaggio did most of his great work before *our* painter was born," Mónica interjected.

"Who cares?" said Cristina. "There's a large painting of a crucified Christ by Zurbarán in the church, and the metal cross on that little stone fountain is said to be designed by him, about four hundred years ago."

"Amazing."

(Shortly before I began to write this, the cross was broken off by vandals, then found and replaced a week or so later, possibly because the culprits had been threatened with lengthy prison sentences for desecrating such an important piece of patrimony.)

"Do you know the Grand Canyon?" Cristina asked me.

"Er, I have seen it on television."

"A man from Llerena found it."

"Really?"

"Yes, García López de Cárdenas y Figueroa was a conquistador who was exploring the Colorado region in 1540 when they arrived at the top of the canyon. They were unable to get down to have a drink in the river, so they had to return to their base due to dehydration," she said as if she were relating what a neighbour had done the day before, but I understood her crisp diction, which was the main thing.

By then night was falling and Cristina suggested a quick drink in a nearby bar before going to the family home. We concurred and when she ordered a whisky and water, Mónica asked her if their father was being especially tiresome.

She sipped, sighed, and sipped again. "No more than usual, but I'm glad you're home, and Juanjo is too, as he's looking forward to seeing more of me. He's so grateful, in fact, that he's prepared a car for you to use for the time being, until you buy your own."

Mónica sipped her coffee. "That's very kind of him. Will he be dining with us later?"

"Oh, I doubt it. He and mother have fallen out again."

"I see. About the usual thing?"

"Yes."

"What is that?" I asked.

"Their religious differences," Cristina said, before slowly explaining that as Juanjo had been an altar boy and had shown some signs of a priestly vocation in his teens, it saddened their mother that he now only attended church at Easter, solely because he took part in the procession which accompanied the statue of the Virgin Mary around town.

"I see. And do you go to church, Cristina?"

"Rarely. Hardly any of us do, and she seems resigned to this, as at least we're respectful, unlike… some people, but as Juanjo is a member of La Hermandad de Nuestro Padre Jesús Nazareno, she does nag him so about attending church more regularly."

"Ah."

She chuckled. "In the Easter fraternities most of them just enjoy dressing up in their robes, parading around, and eating and drinking a lot, but our mother fails to understand this. Fortunately she won't annoy you about religious matters at all."

"Ah, good, but why not?"

"Well, being a Protestant, you're basically a heathen in her eyes, little better than a Muslim or a Hindu."

"Oh." I looked at Mónica. "You didn't mention this."

She smiled. "Don't be alarmed. Our mother respects the beliefs of others, generally speaking. All Cristina means is that religion simply won't be an issue with you, unless… hmm…"

"What?"

"Well, you'd better take care not to show any signs of devotion, as we sometimes do, or she may come to see you as a lost sheep who might be saved. Then, before you know it, you'll be sitting with the priest, receiving religious instruction."

Cristina crossed herself. "Don't do this, for instance."

"Or bow your head when she says grace."

I slurped my beer and sighed. "But to bow the head is only showing respect. What can I do? Stare at you all?"

Cristina patted my hand. "Just observe something on the table. That way your head is inclined, but you aren't praying."

"Vale."

"When Juanjo does that, it drives her crazy."

I finished my small glass of beer and began to wring my hands. "Now I am getting nervous. I don't want to offend your mother."

Mónica squeezed my writhing knuckles. "Oh, you needn't worry about mother at all. She's a saint, really."

Cristina placed her empty glass on the table. "She must be. Shall we have another drink?"

Mónica shook her head. "No, come on, it's time to go home."

By this time it was becoming quite chilly, and as we drove around the one-way system to the house, two streets back from the square, we saw many more people around, most of them well wrapped up for their Saturday night out.

"I believe it gets quite cold here in winter," I said.

"Oh, it freezes less than it used to," said Cristina. "And here in the south, almost in Andalucia, it isn't as cold as the rest of Extremadura, where nocturnal temperatures of minus ten aren't uncommon in midwinter."

"And here we get many quite warm, sunny winter days," said Mónica. "Perfect for our walks. Oh, look at that funny old car."

I smiled at the ancient Citroen Dyane whose bright green paint appeared to have been applied by hand.

Cristina parked up behind it. "Yes, it's the only one that Juanjo can spare right now. It's perfectly reliable, he says."

Mónica nodded doubtfully. "Please thank him for us."

This proved to be unnecessary, because presently a handsome, well-built fellow with wavy grey hair emerged from the studded wooden door opposite, crossed the narrow street, opened the boot, and began to carry the cases inside. I quickly climbed out to greet and assist him.

"Hola, Juanjo, soy Brian," I said on intercepting him on his return from the lobby.

He squeezed my outstretched hand while reaching for another case. "Hola, Brian. Welcome to Llerena. Come to our house whenever you wish." He trotted inside with a case and a rucksack, before taking the keys which dangled from Cristina's fingers, kissing her on the forehead, hugging and kissing Mónica, and jumping into the now empty Merc. "Good luck, Brian!" he hollered in English, before speeding away along the street.

"He is in a hurry," I observed.

"Meeting his friends, no doubt," said Cristina.

"And successfully avoiding his future brother-in-law's introduction to Don Andrés," Mónica said with a smile.

"Will it be so bad?" I enquired as I viewed the whitewashed façade of the large house which blended in with the neighbouring abodes.

"We'll soon see." She ushered me inside and the heavy door clicked shut behind us.

6

Beyond a small outer lobby and under the bright lights of an electric chandelier, I feasted my eyes on a large marble-floored area leading to an impressive staircase with a shiny wooden banister atop an intricate wrought iron railing which curved around the wide tiled steps.

"Wow," I couldn't help but say, because a whole floor of my house would have fit into that essentially unused space. I gazed around at the dark marble wall tiles.

"Don't look for a lift, Brian," said Cristina. "Because despite our father's infirmities they won't let us install one. It's a protected building, and although it's seen many alterations in the last two or three centuries, nowadays we aren't allowed to change a thing."

"I see. It's a lovely... vestibule."

Mónica pointed out a door tucked inconspicuously under the rising staircase. "Through there you'll find the servants' quarters."

"Oh. Are there many of them?"

Cristina laughed. "None have lived here during our lifetime. Nowadays the family members who like to be tranquil stay in those poky rooms when they come to visit, and more recently at our brother Edu's modern house on the edge of town."

Mónica intercepted a question that she saw I was about to ask Cristina. "At holiday times Juanjo also has relatives to stay, so none of ours fit in their house."

"At Christmas the population of Llerena increases a lot," Cristina said as she wiped a few specks of dust from the banister. "Ah, so many years of poverty have turned our little town into a place of pilgrimage, as everybody who wishes to get on in life has to leave."

"Except you," said Mónica. "With your nice safe job at the town hall."

She smiled. "Yes, well, I settled for my lovely local man." She frowned. "Though I sometimes wish he weren't such an unsociable devil. Come on, let's get these cases upstairs."

On the second of the three floors, far less space had been wasted and I soon stepped through a ten-foot-high doorway into a lengthy, wood-panelled passage with ornate lights overhead and a few old paintings on the walls. Realising that the staircase had ended at the door, I asked them how the third floor was accessed.

"Up some stairs along there," said Cristina. "Shall we show him his bedroom now?" she asked her sister.

Mónica smiled sheepishly. "Er, I hoped to discuss the sleeping arrangements later on, once we've seen the lie of the land."

"Oh, so will we not be sleeping together?" I murmured.

She pointed at a wooden cross on the wall below a small picture of the Virgin Mary. "Over my mother's dead body," she said in English.

"Oh."

She patted my cheek. "But don't worry, because I have a plan," she said in Spanish.

"Ah, bien."

Seeing my downcast expression, Cristina gave me a friendly dig in the ribs. "In the main house alone there are eight bedrooms, and over the years, or even the centuries, there have been no end of nocturnal perambulations as unmarried lovers have sought each other out, so your situation is nothing new, believe me."

"Vale."

"And I absolutely forbade mother from putting you in the old servants' quarters as she initially suggested. I told her that you're a fine English gentleman, used to a spacious room with a large bed."

I had to laugh, so I did.

"Quién va allí!" boomed a distant, echoey, male voice, meaning, as you may know or have guessed, who goes there?

"He sounds well," said M.

"He's excited about meeting Brian," said C.

Brian just gulped.

A distant door creaked open, and in a scene somehow reminiscent of an Edgar Allan Poe tale, a corpulent figure began to hobble towards us, breathing heavily as he jabbed a wooden stick into the long, threadbare carpet runner. I was mildly surprised to see him wearing a three-piece tweed suit and carpet slippers, but it was his florid face which grabbed my attention. Below an abundant shock of grey hair, a noble forehead led my eyes down to his watery bloodshot ones, a large mottled nose, a handsome grey moustache, and a sensuous mouth full of yellowed teeth which were almost all exposed in the falsest smile I'd ever seen in my life. His double chin wobbled as he began to guffaw in an endearing way, before he extended a slightly shaky right hand which I pressed with a moderate degree of firmness.

He gazed into my eyes. "So this is the famous Englishman who has won my favourite daughter's heart," he enunciated clearly, thank goodness.

Not sure if he was speaking to me directly, I ventured a nod.

"And does he speak?"

I nodded.

"Answer him, Brian," said his favourite daughter. "He deliberately addresses people in that silly way to unsettle them."

"Be quiet, you little tell-tale," he said, before absently kissing her cheek. "Well, Brian, when I was told that Mónica had snared a fine Englishman, I feared that I wouldn't live long enough to meet you, but as you can see, the miracles of medicine have restored my health to some extent."

"I believe you were suffering from gout, Don Andrés," I was bold enough to say, using the formal 'usted' form of speech.

He giggled, or rather gurgled. "You may tutear me, Brian, and skip the Don, please, as I'm sure you and I will become great friends."

"I hope so... Andrés."

He smiled more sincerely and squeezed my shoulder. "Come, the head of the household is waiting to meet you."

He led us past several closed doors and pushed open a larger one at the end of the passage. Within I saw a splendid chandelier above a lengthy dining table covered by a finely embroidered cloth. The chilly oblong room contained a total of twenty chairs, six of them more or less cushioned and arranged around a large, empty hearth. There were several old paintings on the walls, all landscapes apart from two fine portraits.

"An enchanting room," I said.

He smoothed the tablecloth and sighed. "We only use it for our family gatherings. Nowadays our household is small and impoverished."

"Oh." Expecting one of the ladies to chip in, I realised that they'd both slipped away. Beyond the large windows I spied a darkened patio, so I remarked that the house was much larger than it appeared from the street.

"Well, we Llerenenses are known for our modesty. Aside from the returning conquistadors, who built fine palaces with their booty, the lesser gentry preferred their houses to be deep rather than wide. On this old street and others many have been turned into apartments, and this place will no doubt suffer the same fate once we've died. With no central heating, you'll now see how we've adapted to circumstances. Ah, when I was a child there was always a roaring fire in here in wintertime, but, alas, the price of firewood now makes this ruinous."

I glanced at the portraits. "Are they your parents?"

He pointed at the elaborate, high-collared dress and grinned.

"Or your grandparents?"

"Ha, ha, look more closely at the clothes."

I trawled my recently enlarged lexicon for the right word. "Your... great-grandparents?" (Bisabuelos.)

"That's more like it, but they, my dear Brian, are my great-great-grandparents." (Tatarabuelos.)

"Wow."

He pointed at the man who stood erectly in a peaked cap, frock coat and breeches, gazing into the distance. "Observe the innumerable oak trees and the shadow of the house which my ancestor modestly left out of the picture." He shuffled along to the other portrait. "Now, see the wheat fields, with peasants toiling in the distance, and the shadow of a house depicted in a similarly tantalising way. Alas, I saw neither of those country retreats, as they were both demolished long before my time."

"So I suppose yours was a very wealthy family."

"Oh, no wealthier than several others here. We had a few thousand hectares and three or four houses, none of them especially grand. I believe our failing was that hardly any of us tried our luck in the Americas. We merely clung to our land through the generations, but when the workers began to leave for the cities, especially after the Civil War, it became clear that our way of life was doomed. Now we own just a few useless hectares that I lease to a goatherd for a pittance." He shrugged and smiled at his great-great-grandfather. "How the mighty have fallen, eh?"

"Times change," I said philosophically, electing not to mention that he'd represented an agricultural machinery firm for many years, performing a role not unlike my own. If he wished to play the impoverished landowner, that was all right by me, and the fact that he seemed to regard me sympathetically came as a great relief, because the image of the bedridden tyrant which Mónica had depicted now seemed a tad exaggerated.

"Times do indeed change, my friend. Now let us enter the squalid reality of our life."

He pushed open a door opposite the hearth and showed me into a cosy parlour where a graceful grey-haired lady sat at the head of a large oval table, flanked by her doting daughters. Still a handsome woman in her mid-seventies, my prospective mother-in-law extracted herself from the tablecloth which reached the floor and approached me with her hand outstretched.

I pressed it lightly. "Pleased to meet you, Doña Luisa," I said, once again using the formal form of address.

"Welcome, Brian. I hope your stay with us will be a pleasant one. Please take a seat and dinner will be served shortly."

"Gracias." After getting tangled up in the heavy tablecloth, Mónica pulled it onto my lap and I felt the warmth of the under-table heater placed in the centre of a wooden platform, a traditional heating method – previously using embers from the fireplace rather than electricity – which I'd never experienced before.

"Good chat with my dad?" she murmured in English.

"Yes, fine."

She squeezed my hand. "He must like you."

"I think he might."

"Now, now, you two!" the man in question boomed in Spanish, which came as a shock after his far softer tones in the other room. "No gossiping in foreign tongues, ha ha."

"Perdón, Don Andrés."

"Just Andrés to you."

"Sí, Andrés," I said, wondering if Doña Luisa might ask me to drop the Doña and the 'usted' form, but she just smiled amiably, before raising a tiny bell and giving it a shake.

"Oh, Mamá, will you never learn?" Cristina wailed, before leaving the room by another door, closely followed by Mónica.

I glanced enquiringly at Don Andrés, who I prefer to refer to with the prefix, as I soon found that most of the townsfolk used it, albeit jocosely in some cases. He nodded toward the door.

"Go and take a look at the servants, slaving away over the boiling cauldrons."

"Oh…"

"You needn't bother, Brian," Doña Luisa said amiably.

"Go on, go on," Don Andrés insisted, shooing me to my feet. "You might as well see what goes on behind the scenes of our opulent life." He cackled. "Eh, dear?"

She shrugged, grimaced, and was rubbing the cross around her neck when I left the room.

In the large, functional kitchen I was introduced to Alicia, a swarthy lady in her thirties who Mónica told me was the cook and only the cook.

"Pay no attention to that damned bell if she rings it," Cristina said as she arranged some strips of cured ham on a plate. "Her legs function perfectly well."

"But what if Don Andrés is ill or something?" the cook said while stirring the contents of a deep frying pan.

"Then he'll bellow like a bull, no doubt. You needn't step out of the kitchen much at all if you don't want to, Alicia. We don't want to lose you, like the others."

"Oh, I don't mind seeing what your mother wants."

Cristina turned to Mónica and me. "Alicia's been here for about three weeks, making tasty lunches almost every day and also returning to prepare the occasional dinner. The last cook, a mature lady who was accustomed to the old ways, ignored my advice and paid attention to the bell. At first it was a tinkle here and a tinkle there, usually for food-related reasons, but once mother got back into the habit, poor Carmen responded as readily as one of Pavlov's dogs and found herself performing tasks all over the house, including cleaning the bath in which the cleaner had failed to notice a few of father's pubic hairs."

Alicia blushed even more deeply than I did, but only she received a reassuring pat on the arm.

"I believe Carmen woke up one day and realised that her simple job had turned into an exhausting affair that she felt too old to go on doing, so she regretfully handed in her notice after lasting almost a year. So, Alicia, be warned."

"Vale, Cristina."

"You can go home soon."

I began to lend a hand and as we bustled around I asked Mónica in English if her mother, supposedly a saintly woman, didn't realise that bell-tinkling came across as a bit Victorian and was hardly the done thing in these days of supposed equality. She explained that Mamá's fine forebears – who believed themselves to be descendants of Pedro Cieza de León, a conquistador who wrote a lengthy chronicle about his adventures in Peru – had still been lording it over their servants when she was a girl. Although she'd come down to earth a bit after her marriage, those formative years had left their mark and the Battle of the Bell, a family heirloom, had been going on intermittently for years.

"She means no harm," Mónica concluded in Spanish.

"Where the devil is that food!" my new pal Andrés bellowed from the parlour.

"*He* is the troublesome one."

Having generally found first impressions to be a fairly accurate indication of things to come, I saw myself favouring the droll Don Andrés over his strait-laced wife, but as I deftly uncorked a bottle of red wine I warned myself not to jump to conclusions.

After grace had been said without incident, despite Don Andrés pretending to pick his nose, our nine o'clock dinner proved to be an entertaining affair. As we tucked into the traditional Migas – pan-fried bread with bits of meat and veg – Mónica told her family about our whirlwind romance, omitting any reference to cohabitation, and I was interrogated subtly by Doña Luisa regarding my provenance and career. Meanwhile, Don Andrés concentrated on stuffing himself with Migas, ham, cheese, fried squid, anchovies, saucy meatballs, garlicky potatoes, and, I believe, a single slice of tomato from the abundant salad. He washed all this down with several small glasses of wine and I was surprised that the ladies didn't pull him up about this gastronomical debauch so soon after his almost fatal attack of gout.

Having only paid a flying visit home in August, Mónica was eager to hear the latest family news, so Cristina began to work her way through the siblings, from the youngest, Alejandro, in Monchengladbach, through Felipe in Salamanca, Lourdes in Cáceres, herself in Llerena, Alberto in Badajoz, Mari Carmen in Madrid, to Edu in Barcelona. I paid close attention to her informative discourse, wishing I had a notebook, as most of their thirteen children were out in the world, doing more or less interesting things.

Doña Luisa wasn't impressed that Lourdes had filed for divorce from her husband, an industrial chemist, as despite his serial philandering she insisted that the marriage vows were sacred. Nor was she too chuffed about Edu's only son Marco having become something of a Catalan nationalist, as she believed that Spain should remain united, no matter what these misguided radicals aspired to.

Don Andrés nudged my arm. "She wishes the Caudillo was still alive."

"The... oh, do you mean Franco?"

"The same." He turned to his wife. "Everyone knew their place in those days, didn't they, dear?"

Her fine brown eyes narrowed. "You liked him well enough in your youth, Francisco, when you were proud to have been named after the Generalísimo."

He shrugged. "We knew no better in those days. Only later did it come to light that the Nationalists had executed many Republican prisoners here during the Civil War, and hundreds more in Badajoz. Most of the witnesses were dead or had fled, and the rest remained mute."

She tutted. "The Reds were even worse, murdering innocent priests and nuns."

"Not around here." He turned to me. "At first the workers and peasants took control and locked up plenty of people like us, including two of my wife's uncles, but not a single one was killed."

Doña Luisa had laid down her fork and picked up her rosary beads. "Only because they didn't have time. I'm sure Brian isn't interested in these depressing old stories."

I was, but I knew the time wasn't ripe to delve into matters which hardly anyone had wished to discuss during my two years in Valencia. Since then a tacit agreement to forget had been superseded by a desire to discover the mass graves which had been filled with victims during those three appalling years when neither side had bothered with POW camps, but I digress, because Mónica had already nipped this irksome topic in the bud and was asking Cristina about Alberto's recent sideways move within the Badajoz Provincial Council.

The brother who had been speaking so loudly on the phone when I'd first met her in Clitheroe had been transferred from his executive post dealing with sewage to one somehow related to rural tourism, but Cristina didn't know much about his new role.

"I'll speak to him soon," said Mónica. "Brian and I are very interested in the possibilities of rural tourism in the Campiña Sur," she said, referring to the administrative area in the south-east of the province of which Llerena is the capital. (Not to be confused with the Campiña Sur of Cordoba, a larger but inferior sort of place, she later told me.) With a population of thirty thousand spread over about twenty municipalities, this explained why Llerena was such a thriving little town, as many villagers came to shop, perform administrative tasks, and avail themselves of the modest hospital, unless their condition was especially grave, in which case they'd be driven or flown to Badajoz.

"Aren't we, Brian?"

"Oh, sí. El turismo rural es muy interesante," I concurred.

"What is it?" said Doña Luisa.

"Tourism in the countryside, Mamá."

"Plenty of tourists come here in summer," said Cristina.

"Yes, but only a few spend the night in the area. They come here, take photos in the square, then move on to one of the cities. I know we have a lovely hotel and another cheaper one, and in town and elsewhere there are houses and apartments for rent, so Brian and I are interested in becoming involved in this too."

Cristina mentioned a rural hotel in a fine old farmhouse a few kilometres away, set in acres of land with a well-regarded restaurant, a large swimming pool, and horses to ride.

Mónica smiled. "Ah, yes, I know it. I'd love to own a place like that."

I almost choked on half an artichoke, and after Don Andrés had slapped me on the back I averted my startled eyes from Mónica's eager ones, because her aspirations appeared to be rising by the hour. Having only just retired from my demanding job, I fancied at least a few weeks of downtime in which to familiarise myself with my new home, before looking into the sort of business options that mature folk generally consider. Buying a house with an appendage which could be rented out appealed to me, or, due to my knowhow, perhaps a little furniture trafficking of one kind or another. I'd even mused on the idea of us simply doing a bit of informal teaching to keep the Iberian wolf from the door, but I'd been forgetting that Mónica wasn't yet fifty and seemed to have a strong desire to become an entrepreneur after so many years of clocking in at a secondary school.

"Unfortunately, a real hotel will be too expensive for us," I said after noticing that all eyes were upon me.

Mónica patted my hand. "One never knows what might be possible, but there'll be time enough to talk about it."

"Brian thought he'd come here to take it easy, ha ha," said the perceptive Don Andrés.

After we'd cleared away the plates and shoved them in the dishwasher, Cristina made a pot of coffee, but despite the potency of the brew, a collective drowsiness soon assailed us. Presently Cristina offered to show me to my room, a task which I'd assumed Mónica would do, but after I'd bidden their parents buenas noches and kissed my girlfriend on the cheek, on the way up the stairs Cristina assured me that we were merely adhering to the usual protocol.

"Mónica will join you in a while and she'll spend the night with you here," she said after we'd entered a chilly room with a regular double bed.

"Vale, but your mother might find out."

She switched on a small convector heater. "Oh, no, she never finds out."

"Never?"

"No, or not for many, many years. Despite her piety, deep down she's a realist. Tonight she wouldn't dream of entering Mónica's room, only two doors from her own, because she knows she won't be there. For as long as you stay here, every evening you two will say goodnight and retire separately. You'll also arrive at the breakfast table separately, if only by a few moments." She shrugged. "C'est la vie in the house of a mature Catholic lady, I'm afraid."

"Oh, I don't mind," said the mature (lapsed) Protestant gentleman who couldn't see himself living under the proposed regime for longer than he had to. I hadn't retired early and flown abroad with my beloved only to spend my time hoodwinking my future mother-in-law, and nor did I relish the prospect of eating most of my meals with her.

Cristina squeezed my arm. "I'll wish you goodnight and go home now, Brian."

"Yes, goodnight, and thank you for everything."

She smiled sleepily. "I'm glad you and Mónica have come home. Finally I'll be able to spend more time with Juanjo."

"I'm glad. Does he not often enter the house?"

"Oh, yes, on the Day of the Kings, Good Friday, and a few more times when the family is gathered here."

"I see."

She shrugged. "Other brothers and sisters-in-law enjoy spending time here, partly because my parents pay for everything, but Juanjo has established certain boundaries. He has a family, after all, and he likes his independence." She chuckled. "His views differ from those of my mother too, him being of more working-class origins, so I suppose it's all for the best."

I was about to hint that I didn't wish to become a fixture in the house either, but not wishing to seem ungrateful for their hospitality, I saw her out, cleaned my teeth in the adjacent bathroom, and soon climbed into bed after leaving the door ajar for my lover.

At least we have the third floor to ourselves, I thought as I browsed through a breviary which I'd found on the bedside table.

7

At about half past eight the following morning I found Mónica alone in the kitchen, preparing breakfast for the four of us. She hadn't made it up to my room because after a lengthy bedside chat with her mother – her parents had slept in separate rooms for many years – she'd thought it disrespectful to violate her old-fashioned norms on the very first night.

"I was about to fetch you a cup of tea," she said brightly, looking very much at home in the airy kitchen, and ravishing in her pretty polka-dot apron. As she arranged a tray I embraced her and playfully nibbled her left ear.

"Ooh, stop it, Brian. Mamá might come in."

I desisted and toddled off with the cutlery which the recently seated Don Andrés found wanting, due to the absence of knives and forks.

"This is what Mónica told me to bring."

"How am I supposed to eat my sausages, son?"

Not having seen or smelt any evidence of frying, I told him I'd go and ask.

"Papá's diet begins today," Mónica told me. "So we can expect a lively breakfast."

"Vale."

"Cristina's indulged him for too long. She's allowed him to keep a stash of sausages which he's been frying for his breakfast, but as I don't wish to become his nurse, his cholesterol consumption is going to decrease radically. Alicia already has a new shopping list."

"Vale."

She stroked my cheek and smiled. "Just bear with me for a few days until things settle down."

"I will."

After she'd assured me that we'd be free to do as we pleased between breakfast and dinner, we trooped into the sitting room with the boxes of cereals, jugs of milk and apple juice, a large fruit salad, and little else. We found Doña Luisa mumbling the rosary and Don Andrés sniffing the air.

His eyes alighted on the trays. "For whom is all that muck?"

Mónica informed him that he'd be eating a healthy breakfast from then on.

"Ni muerto!" he cried, which translates roughly as 'over my dead body'.

"It's precisely your death that we wish to avoid," she said sternly. "Isn't that so, Mamá?"

"Holy Mary, Mother of God, pray for us sinners, now and at the hour of our death. Amen," she muttered, before crossing herself. "That's right," she said more clearly. "It's a sin to gorge yourself on fatty food in your condition."

"Bah, only a venial one."

"Suicide is a mortal sin, Papá."

He growled as he grabbed the cornflakes box and shook a few into his bowl, before examining the milk jar. "What's this supposed to be, cow's piss?"

"It's skimmed milk, Andrés," I said, amused by his turn of phrase.

He glared at his daughter. "My God, life won't be worth living while you're around to bully me. Brian, you'd better start looking for a house or a hotel to buy right away, or you'll also end up being reduced to skin and bones."

I patted my somewhat reduced paunch. "I am also on a diet, Andrés, so I will have… solidarity with you."

"Oh, madre mía!" He forced a few cornflakes down. "Hmm, well, I suppose this crap will keep me going until lunchtime. What'll we be having today?"

"A vegetarian paella," said Mónica.

"Me cago en la leche!" he yelled, meaning, I shit myself in the milk, a common turn of phrase in Spanish which still sounds harsh to my ears, although many people use it with different nouns such as the whore, the whore mother, your ancestors, or even God.

His face crimson and with skimmed milk dribbling down his chin, he glared at me and pointed at the door. "Brian, today you must get out there and find a place to live where you can put my daughter in her place. Here, under the pious eyes of my wife, you'll end up as emasculated as I've become."

I chuckled indulgently, because his light-hearted harangue suited me well. Aware that it would take time to find a house, even to rent, the sooner we began to make enquiries the better, as Christmas was only just over a month away and I was eager to vacate the family mansion before then. Over my Spanish weetabix, upon which I was permitted to pour a little honey, I expressed interest in seeing the Zurbarán painting in the church.

Doña Luisa smiled at me warmly. "Ah, yes, Our Lady of Granada is the finest church for miles around and it's well worth spending some time there. It will be quiet there soon, so you might wish to sit for a while and enjoy the sacred atmosphere of our Lord's house while viewing the magnificent gilded altarpiece."

"Vale."

Don Andrés cackled in anticipation of what he was about to say. "Yes, and afterwards you ought to visit the history museum."

When Doña Luisa groaned, I wondered if I might find some nude statues there.

"We'll visit everywhere eventually, Papá."

Don Andrés cleared his throat. "Ah, yes, the history museum, in the building which was once the… episcopal palace."

"Ah, how interesting."

"Yes, a fine fifteenth century structure which later became… do you wish to tell him, dear?"

Doña Luisa raised her eyes to the mini-chandelier and sighed. "Why bother? Your heretical point of view will only end up polluting Brian's mind anyway."

Don Andrés gleefully rubbed his hands together. "At the episcopal palace in the late fifteenth century, the nice bishop began to pull a few strings and some of his pals from Toledo came up with the idea of establishing the Court of the Holy Office of the Inquisition right here in Llerena. It was the third largest in Spain and they got to work on the Hebraic settlements in southern Extremadura right away, packing the men off to row the king's ships, if they were lucky, though they were normally tortured and burnt to death. The poor Moriscos got the worst of it though, as many of them were quite rich, so if the Inquisition got so much as a whiff of Islamic practices, they'd get a couple of hundred lashes for starters, then meet the same fate as the Jews."

"How awful," I said, striving to keep a straight face, as Don Andrés was clearing laying it on thick for my benefit.

"And as for any of those new-fangled Protestants who were foolish enough to head south of the Pyrenees to try to convert us lot, well, they tried out *all* their methods of torture on those misguided fools, before putting what was left of them on the bonfire." He tipped back his head and inhaled deeply through his nostrils. "Ah, though I haven't had my sausages, I can still smell the stench of burning flesh only a few streets from here."

Doña Luisa gazed at me sadly as her strong teeth decimated a few cornflakes. "Please take his gross exaggeration with a pinch of salt, Brian. I only hope that he'll repent and confess to his many sins while there's still time. Deep down he's a good man, and the Lord may yet spare him eternal damnation."

Don Andrés nudged me. "She keeps a thumbscrew under her pillow, for old times' sake, ha ha."

"That's enough now, Papá. I'm glad to see you in such good spirits, but please try to be more considerate."

Doña Luisa then said something that I won't forget in a hurry.

"It's true that the Inquisition used barbaric methods, but people were generally more bloodthirsty in those days. Nowadays we've reached the opposite extreme. All kinds of foreigners come to Spain without money or skills and many neighbourhoods in the cities are now full of them. They procreate and don't integrate, and although my views are considered old-fashioned, I can't help but pine for the times when Spain was a truly united nation."

"Don't talk rubbish, Luisa," Don Andrés snapped. "Spain's never been united and you know it."

Mónica slapped his hand. "Hey, you provoked her in the first place. Don't lose your sense of humour now."

He growled before lowering his head and savaging a spoonful of fruit salad.

Just then – excuse a little poetic licence here, as in reality this didn't occur until the following day – I heard a tap on the door and a dusky young lady wearing a headscarf peered around it.

"Señora, shall I clean the upstairs bathroom today, or leave it until Thursday?"

Doña Luisa smiled. "Thursday will be fine, Samira, thank you."

The Moroccan cleaner withdrew and Don Andrés gazed at me dolefully, unable or unwilling to come up with a witticism.

"Samira has been working here for about four years, Brian," her employer said proudly.

"Just before I went to England, my mother bought her a lovely pushchair for her second child," Mónica told me, before shaking her head. "You must think we're a bunch of nutters," she murmured in English.

I raised my hands, a bit like a priest. "All of us… generalise sometimes, but it is our actions that are important," I said sagely in Spanish.

"Amen," said Don Andrés, before pushing himself to his feet. "*I* will make the coffee today."

"That's a first," said the saintly reactionary.

8

By the time we reached the church a fresh congregation was congregating, so we left Zurbarán's Christ for another day and set off on our Sunday walk. Within minutes we reached the edge of town, and after passing the modernistic new bullring which doubles as an auditorium for open-air concerts, we headed south along a dusty track. After a mile or so we began to climb into some scrubby woods that became denser as we approached a vantage point offering great views of the compact town and the flatlands to the north. To the south the rolling wooded hills gradually increased in height and I realised that I was looking at the famous Sierra Morena, a former haunt of bandits and highwaymen, and the place where Don Quixote sought sanctuary after freeing the galley slaves – perchance victims of the Inquisition – from their chains.

Despite the mild sunshine, the wind made it chilly up there, and after over an hour of strenuous hiking I assumed we'd be making tracks back towards the town. Until then we'd chatted about inconsequential matters, but on the way down I intended to suggest putting out a few feelers in order to find a house to rent. Although my maiden breakfast had been entertaining and instructive, I suspected that a dozen more of them would be enough to be going on with, as we'd also be dining with the oddly matched couple who Mónica assured me loved each other dearly, despite their conflicting opinions on almost everything, from astrology through to religious zealotry.

Instead of heading homeward, however, Mónica coaxed me along a ridge to the south and after a while we began to descend a steep, sinuous path towards a village called Casas de Reina. Its white, red-roofed houses were rather like those of Llerena, which I could see some way to the north across the fields. To test the water I said that it might be a pleasant place to live.

"I agree. The population has been falling for decades, from over a thousand to only a couple of hundred, so there are bound to be some properties for sale that might suit us."

"Hmm, perhaps we could rent a place, to see what it's like to live there."

"Perhaps. Can you see that structure some way to the other side of the village?"

"Oh, yes. Is it a farm or something?"

She giggled. "Not quite, though I'm sure many years ago there was at least one farm nearby."

Her giggling unsettled me, so I decided to ask her if she wanted us to buy the structure in question, as I wished to nip any plans of spending a large amount of money in the bud. Although we were still enjoying our honeymoon period, I feared that domestic bliss would be impossible beneath the same roof as her parents, but to go to the other extreme and commit ourselves to the purchase of an expensive property would be madness at such an early stage in our relationship. I worked out how to say all this fluently in Spanish, before pointing at the place and popping the question.

She laughed heartily. "Oh, Brian, not even Bill Gates could buy it."

"Hmm, it must be expensive then."

"Not expensive, but priceless, though it may well have a part to play in our future." Feeling my hand go limp in hers, she squeezed it reassuringly. "Though of course I won't try to pressure you into doing anything unless you're just as keen as me."

"That's good. I hope we'll be able to get a drink and a bite to eat soon," I said, as my legs were already aching and the closer we got to the village, the further away Llerena appeared to be.

By way of reply she unslung her little knapsack and handed me a large bottle of mineral water.

"Gracias, cariño."

"We will stop in the village, but on the way home, as I want us to approach the structure without seeing any signs."

"How intriguing."

She tittered. "I'll be observing your reaction to it, as I believe it may play a crucial role in the idea I have in mind." She squeezed my hand. "And which I hope you'll like."

"I will approach it with an open mind."

"Muy bien."

So we took a series of rough paths to the south of the village and eventually reached a deserted road which we plodded along for a while until I saw a discreet brown sign which gave the game away.

"Oh, a Roman theatre," I said, injecting as much enthusiasm into my voice as I could muster, as I was thoroughly fagged out after about eight miles of walking, not being accustomed to lengthy Peak District hikes like Mónica.

"Yes, a Roman theatre that relatively few people visit, due to it being mentioned only briefly in most of the tourism literature. The regional government prefers to steer people towards Mérida, Cáceres, Trujillo and other towns, where they're likely to stay and spend plenty of money."

"I guess that makes sense."

"Ah, yes, but with my brother Alberto now involved in rural tourism on the provincial council, I hope he'll help us to put this place more firmly on the map."

After passing through some open gates, we wandered along a smooth track, but all I could see on either side were scrubby fields. "Is this… something?"

"All this is yet to be excavated. I'll show you the main attraction first, before we walk around to see the other buildings that have already been unearthed."

"My legs are getting a bit tired," I whined.

"Don't worry, we'll soon find a lovely place to sit down."

"Vale."

As we approached three crumbly ancient walls I affixed a smile to my face, as I was determined not to appear disappointed by the pile of stones I expected to see behind them, but what I beheld was actually quite impressive. The semi-circular seating area was well-preserved, while the stone backdrop to the stage was adorned with a few pillars which no longer propped anything up. I deduced that the stage itself was almost certainly less than two thousand years old, because it was made of wood.

As we stood upon it, imagining a cheering crowd of Roman colonists, Mónica told me that in summer the occasional theatrical production took place there, though the stage served mainly as a platform from which to view the auditorium and take selfies, which a chattering Spanish family proceeded to do as soon as we'd stepped off it.

"So what do you think?" she asked me after we'd taken a pew and begun to scoff some fruit bars.

"It's quite impressive, especially here in the middle of nowhere," I said diplomatically, as the initial thrill had now subsided and couldn't imagine folk flocking there from miles around, not with the awe-inspiring Roman remains of Mérida only an hour's drive away.

"Yes, and this is only part of it. Come on."

So after about four minutes' rest we left through an intact arch and she led me past the unexcavated area to a series of former dwellings, none more than a yard high and most little more than foundations.

"Isn't it atmospheric, Brian?"

I closed my eyes and imagined the smell of sizzling Christians. "Yes, it must have been quite a place."

"Just an outpost of the empire really, built mainly to exploit the nearby mines, but can you believe that most Llerenenses have only been here once in their lives, normally on a school trip?"

Sure that I'd feel no burning desire to hurry back, I nonetheless agreed that it was a shame to pay so little attention to such an amazing historical site right on their doorstep, before sitting on a wall to rest my no less weary legs.

She frowned down at me. "I can tell you're not all that impressed."

Believing partial honesty to be the best policy, and conscious of her desire to accommodate visitors in our future rural lodging, I said that I wasn't sure the site would be a strong enough draw to bring folk flocking to the area.

She scowled at a crisp packet on the ground. "Oh, I see."

"Unless they're archaeology enthusiasts who might wish to, er… stay somewhere rural and sort of be… in the middle between Mérida and… and…"

She smiled. "Italica, the marvellous Roman site near Seville?"

"Yes, that's the one."

"And the Roman temple at Cordoba, not to mention the spectacular Arabic city, Medina Azahara, only a few kilometres from there?"

"Yes, those too."

She clicked her fingers and grinned. "Oh, what a brilliant idea your clumsy attempts to please me have produced." She began to pace restlessly around, apparently unfatigued by our hike. "Yes, it's been said before that Llerena sits in the middle of a triangle formed by those three cities, so we must exploit that to the full. This site will simply be a sort of… thematic magnet to get people to come, but on our website we'll also have lots of information about the really important locations. Hmm, I must speak to Alberto right away."

"What can he do?"

"Nothing just yet, but once we have our property, he can give it a mention in the tourist information that someone in his office is surely producing."

"Er, isn't that nepotism?"

"Yes, it's great, isn't it? Ah, I always knew he'd get out of sewage eventually, and fate has had him transferred to rural tourism."

"Fate, yes," I said, realising that our business options had already been narrowed down to a single sector. This didn't dismay me, if it was what she really wanted, but I was a bit worried about the potential size of the enterprise.

I creaked to my feet. "Let's get some lunch in the village. Then you… we can ask if there are any affordable houses for sale."

She skipped towards me and gave me a hug. "Yes, let's do that. Oh, Brian, fate might have made this a decisive day in our lives."

I sighed contentedly. "Yes, it might."

"Oh, in all the excitement I almost forgot the ruined Moorish castle up there." She pointed at a jagged structure on a hill about a mile away. "Shall we nip up there now?"

I put my tender foot down. "Not today, dear."

9

"You might as well finish me off," I said to Don Andrés a few hours later in the large sitting room as he sat before a roaring fire, polishing a shotgun.

He aimed at the chandelier and pulled the trigger. "I don't have any cartridges for this antique. You look tired out, my boy. What has that energetic daughter of mine been doing to you?"

After I'd told him that she'd made me walk twenty-two kilometres, according to her GPS watch, I went into more detail about our outing, especially the part of it which had occurred during our lunch in the excellent village restaurant, where I'd gorged myself on Migas and a delicious lamb stew, while Mónica had scoffed a mushroom omelette and fried fish. She'd asked José Ángel, the affable owner, about available properties in Casas de Reina, and while I was devouring some scrumptious cakes supplied by the nuns of the Santa Clara convent in Llerena, a youngish chap had joined us. Fede – short for Federico – professed to be a tractor mechanic, but he knew so much about the available properties in the area that I felt sure he did a bit of informal estate agency work on the side.

After he'd enthused about various houses – most of them in need of a lick of paint, he admitted – the coffee cleared my head enough to make me wary of this handsome, upbeat fellow who already appeared to have Mónica under his spell.

Although I felt somewhat rested by then, I insisted that the six-kilometre hike home – along a mercifully smooth track, it turned out – precluded any house-viewing that afternoon. This made my indefatigable girlfriend sulk for a while, until I pointed out that we could return soon in the Citroen Dyane which we had yet to try out.

"Then the walk home was torture. I now have… blisters on my feet."

He gazed at me pensively and leaned closer. "Yes, well, blisters soon heal, but bad decisions can have long-lasting consequences."

"Yes, I know." I heard Mónica chirping to her mother in the next room.

"Push the door to, Brian." I did so. "Now, let's give this matter some thought. I imagine that you haven't retired and come here only to get embroiled in some rural tourism scheme right away, have you?"

"No."

"Mónica, on the other hand, has been mulling over this business for a while now, so it's logical that on arriving home she's longing to put her plan into action." He smoothed his moustache and nodded slowly. "I believe that what you need is some kind of diversionary tactic, in order to steer her thoughts away from a potentially rash decision, such as buying a house without thinking things through."

"She's going to speak to Alberto about promoting tourism in the area, especially the Roman theatre."

He guffawed. "That little thing? Haven't they desecrated it with wooden boards and whatnot?"

I smiled. "Yes. Have you seen it recently?"

"Not for about sixty years. My friends and I used to cycle there sometimes. I recall playing cowboys and Indians in the theatre, as the monks who taught us had only given us a hazy understanding of history, and we were much influenced by the cinema of the time. Hmm, so she's going to speak to Alberto, is she?"

"Sí."

He pulled a small mobile phone from his waistcoat pocket. "Then perhaps I'll speak to him first. Tell me, what is it that *you* want to do in the near future, Brian?"

"Well, I'd like us to rent a small house, not too far from here."

He grinned. "But not too near, eh?"

"Oh, in the town or a nearby village. We need time to get to know each other better."

"Of course you do. This rural tourism thing should be left until you've both found your feet. Mónica hasn't really lived here since she went away to university in Badajoz, so she's out of touch. She's always been a bit pig-headed, so we must divert her thoughts away from this for the time being." He began to press a button on the phone. "This is my private line to our children, for when I wish to avoid censorship. Hmm, Alberto, Alejandro… too far away, as is Edu. Felipe's not much of an ideas man, Lourdes in Cáceres, Mari Carmen will be busy with her little grandkids in Madrid… ah, isn't Lourdes about to divorce that cretinous chemist of hers?"

"I believe so."

"Hmm, and her daughter's away studying, so she might be able to lend us a hand."

"Won't she be busy with her work?" I asked, her being a freelance writer, mostly of magazine articles related to interior design and other household subjects.

He grinned. "Her work is just what I'm thinking about, and I doubt she'll stay in Cáceres for long once she's got shut of that baboon. Perhaps…" He rubbed his forehead vigorously. "No, I need to give this matter my full attention before deciding on the way forward. Now, Brian, do I have your blessing to attempt to occupy Mónica's mind with less… irreversible undertakings?"

I recalled her beaming face when the persuasive chap had been doing his damnedest to flog us a house. "Yes, please try to do that." I pictured the bright green Dyane awaiting us on the street. "Really we ought to travel around a little, visiting people and places, you know."

"Exactly." He cocked an ear. "Judging by the incessant chatter in there, your sister-in-law has arrived, so go and join them while I mull over this vital matter."

"Vale. Gracias, Andrés."

"De nada, Brian."

As I'd feared, Mónica's attentive audience of two were saying nothing to dissuade her from talking herself and me into investing our money in some large, shabby house which we'd buy for a song, before spending the rest of the winter doing it up. Come the spring we'd be ready to advertise our lovely guest rooms to history and archaeology buffs around the globe, she told them while I remained rooted to the spot, astonished by how far ahead of herself she was getting.

Cristina's eyes sparkled as she observed my discomfiture. "Aren't you going to rest your legs, Brian?"

"Sí." I sat down in one of the three vacant armchairs and eased off my slippers to air my aching feet.

"You've worn the poor man out, Mónica," said Doña Luisa. "Make him a drink."

"Of course. A cup of tea, Brian?"

"Sí, por favor."

While she was in the kitchen, Cristina sat down beside me and murmured that Mónica was well-known for her bursts of enthusiasm, such as the one which had led to her being stuck in Manchester for two years, but that I could count on their support to help prevent any precipitous decisions.

"Oh, muchas gracias. Today she is like a young girl with a… not a silly idea, exactly, but we need more time to plan something like this." I nodded towards the wall. "Your father is also thinking of things to… divert her thoughts away from buying a house."

Rather than approving of this paternal involvement, Cristina looked distinctly worried, while her mother reached for her rosary beads.

"Er, is this not a good idea?"

Cristina patted my throbbing thigh. "I'm afraid that when my father decides to help one of us, sometimes the cure can be worse than the disease."

"Oh…"

"Though not always. I'd better find out what he's plotting."

As she stepped into the next room and closed the door, Mónica entered by the other with a mug of tea, making me feel that I was participating in a theatrical farce. This feeling would only grow as the week progressed.

That evening Don Andrés told me that I'd have to keep Mónica safely occupied the following day, as he was putting the final touches to a cunning plan which he hoped we could proceed with on Tuesday. Thus it was that when she finally made it to my room after another late-night chinwag with her mother, instead of the libidinous lover she expected to find, she encountered a man who was simply chewing at the bit to see all that Llerena had to offer.

"Oh, we can visit all the old buildings little by little," she crooned as she stroked what was left of my hair. "I thought we might drive that funny old car to Casas de Reina tomorrow and see if Fede can show us a few of those houses."

"Presumably he'll be working, if he is in fact a tractor mechanic," I said in English.

"En castellano, por favor," she murmured as she nuzzled my neck.

"I'm too tired. No, given your enthusiasm to accommodate history-lovers, I insist on seeing what this pleasant town has to offer in the way of historical monuments and so on," I said, enjoying the fluent sound of my own voice, as so much Spanish talk really had fatigued my brain. "Only by spending a day seeing the sights can I be sure that others will find it rewarding."

She undid a couple of pyjama buttons and stroked my unnecessarily hairy chest. "Yes, we'll have a quick look around, then pop over to the village."

"No, it has to be a leisurely tour, with lunch somewhere appealing, so that we can recommend the itinerary to our prospective guests."

"Hmm, I suppose that makes sense." She squeezed my remaining belly fat. "Oh, I can't wait to buy a place that's not too dear and begin to do it up. I enjoy painting, and you're quite good at DIY, aren't you?"

"Well, I know how to do most things, I suppose."

"Great. It'll be such fun." When her hand strayed lower down, she encountered unexpected flaccidity.

"Oh, Brian, after several days of sleeping apart I thought you'd be more eager to please me."

"I was. I think the mention of DIY has... deflated me. I've never been all that keen on doing a lot of it, you see." I yawned, wondering if a celibate spell might calm her ardour regarding her project, but the flesh is weak and we soon forgot about worldly matters for a while...

"Oh, Brian, everything's going to be fine, you'll see," she said as we lay side by side.

With my passion spent but my love stronger than ever, I agreed that it would. Just then I felt like letting her have her way and even plunging us into debt if she so wished.

10

The following morning, however, on awakening to find myself alone, my desire to suavely apply the brakes to her scheme resurged, so over our healthy breakfast I displayed an inordinate enthusiasm to spend the day as a tourist. Don Andrés – now apparently resigned to eating goats' fodder, as he called it – began to reel off all the attractions the town had to offer while I gratefully jotted them down.

"There's such a thing as too much sightseeing, you know," Mónica grumbled. "But I'm sure we'll get through it all before lunch."

"I am merely thinking of our future guests."

This mollified her for a while, but at the bottom of the stairs when I produced a key that Don Andrés had slipped me, she became impatient.

"Oh, why do you want to see the old servants' quarters now?"

I unlocked the door. "Because it's occurred to me that our guests might like to see how the other half used to live."

I soon concluded that the three poky bedrooms, the small sitting room with a kitchenette, and the cramped bathroom would be of negligible interest to tourists, even if we removed the old tellies, the microwave oven, and other appurtenances that family members had added during recent decades. This didn't stop me from exploring every inch of the place, peering into cupboards, under dusty bedspreads, and even trying out the old-fashioned taps.

"Oh, come on, Brian."

"Hey, perhaps we could live here for a while, then we wouldn't have to pay any rent," I remarked, mainly to remind her of our initial plan which she appeared to have forgotten.

"Why the devil would we want to live in this dump with hardly any windows?"

I smiled innocently. "To save money, by not paying rent."

"Who said anything about paying rent?"

"We did. Not so long ago we intended to rent a house at first, as we agreed that to buy a place right away might be a little premature."

"Did we?"

"Yes, during the train journey here, in fact."

"Hmm, well, perhaps we did, but don't you think that renting would be such a waste of money, considering we've got this whole house almost to ourselves?"

It then occurred to me that as Don Andrés and I were getting on like a house on fire, and Doña Luisa appeared to have accepted me to some extent, it would indeed pain me to shell out a monthly amount on a dwelling that would never be ours. Spotting this moment of weakness, Mónica soon steered me outside and tried to bundle me into the bright green car, but I was having none of it.

"Take me to Zurbarán's crucified Christ," I commanded, so she led me briskly to the square, where I perused a fine old statue of my new favourite painter with his brush and palette at the ready.

The interior of the lofty old church was very ornate, especially the altarpiece, and I was soon peering through some bars at Zurbarán's eerily realistic work which Mónica told me he'd painted several times, there being examples of similar canvases in at least three important museums. After having a peek at a couple of elaborate little chapels, I wished to take a pew and soak up the sacred atmosphere, but Mónica soon lured me up some stairs to view the splendid square from one of the many arches, before ignoring a no entry sign and hustling me down a darker stairway and out to a much smaller square.

"You know the church well."

"I came here for years, until after my confirmation I began to know my own mind and only came occasionally to please mother. Right, next stop the convent."

At the Santa Clara convent one is supposed to book a visit, but Mónica sweettalked an elderly nun into allowing us to pass through a lovely porticoed square to see their church with its amazing frescos, before we bought a couple of cakes at their bakery shop and hit the streets again. After strolling along a more modern thoroughfare, munching a heart-shaped pastry, I was surprised to come across the substantial remains of the mighty fourteenth-century town walls, about thirty feet high and with a sizeable tower. In a small park behind it I admired a charming, elongated pond in the Moorish style, and from there the scale of the lengthy stretch of wall could be more readily appreciated. Llerena had been a real fortress town, as although the Moors had been practically ejected from Spain by then, the Order of Saint James – a military as well as religious organisation – ruled the roost and were clearly a security conscious bunch of knights.

As Mónica had been hurrying me from place to place, I became concerned that our tour would be over long before lunchtime, so when she reminded me that three of the four gateways to the town were still intact, I insisted on seeing them all.

"Oh, but why now, Brian? It's far better for you to come across them one by one. That way your sense of surprise and awe will be greater."

"I want to see them now, to situate them strategically in my mind," I droned, before flicking my sheet of notes. "To the Puerta de Reina, por favor."

"Oh, all right."

That ancient stone gateway is now incongruously jammed between two rows of houses, but I dutifully took a photo on my phone, before making a beeline for a little park I'd seen, as I wished to rest my blistered feet for a while. There I was allowed to relax and scoff the other heart-shaped cake which my healthy girlfriend didn't want, but when she began to speak of those dratted village houses again, I pulled her to her feet and we resumed our tour of the gates. These were situated to the south, west and north of the centre, the eastern one having been demolished long before the town's worthies realised that they might be worth preserving for posterity.

Mónica wasn't born yesterday, however, and knowing full well that I was playing for time, she interspersed our route to the other two gates – both noble structures seemingly plonked down in the modern world rather than surrounded by it – with lightning visits to two more churches and three old palaces, the sixteenth-century Palacio de los Zapata, now home to the law courts, being the best of the bunch. By now it was after twelve and my guide believed that she was nearing the end of her task, but I still had a trump card up my sleeve, the history museum housed within the old episcopal palace.

There, spread over two floors around a delightful patio, we saw a host of mostly underwhelming exhibits including pottery, modern artwork, ancient bells, contemporary basketwork, old kitchen utensils, weighing scales, sundry statues, and so on, all of which I perused at length. The things which most appealed to me were the truly permanent exhibits, a series of old wall paintings on religious themes, some of which were remarkably well-preserved.

"Ooh, and look at that writing down there," I said to my fidgety partner. "What's that?"

"Sixteenth century graffiti. It's a biblical proverb in Latin."

"And what does it say?"

"Heavy is the stone, and the sand is heavy, but the anger of the fool is heavier than both."

"Ah, wise words." I kissed her cheek. "Thanks for being so patient. Shall we go and get some lunch now?"

"Sí, por favor."

On this investigative tour only the most splendid eatery would do, so we adjourned to the four-star Hospedería Mirador de Llerena. Although the hotel's restaurant was by no means the best in town, the setting was charming, as they'd done an excellent job of turning a noble nineteenth-century house with a fine patio into a great place to stay which wouldn't break the bank. At only about €100 a night for a double room and with access to a covered swimming pool and jacuzzies, I told Mónica that it was a snip at the price.

"Hmm, well, it's more expensive in summer," she muttered, having guessed the gist of what I was about to say next.

"We'd find it hard to compete with a place like this, or that country hotel with horses that Cristina mentioned."

She speared a spear of asparagus and waved it at me. "No defeatist talk, please. Besides, our place will be far cheaper and more homely than this, with the countryside right on our doorstep."

I stirred my thick potato and red pepper soup. "Oughtn't we to consider other less… complicated options too, love?"

"Such as?"

"Oh, we could offer private English classes, or… something like that," I said, as by then I'd gone off the idea of dealing in furniture, as it might take me ages to learn the ropes and would be too much like my old work.

"Here the council provides cheap English classes, and in the villages there'll be little demand due to the aging population. Besides, I don't wish to ply my trade for a measly few euros an hour… unless, hmm, I think you've given me an idea."

I gulped down a slice of spud and remained silent, because the impious look in her eyes boded ill for my peace of mind.

"In a few months you'll be speaking Castilian fluently, and your accent is unusually good for an Englishman."

"Gracias."

"Yes, so rather than giving English classes to the stingy locals, we could offer courses of immersive Spanish tuition to our affluent foreign guests."

"Oh, God. All roads appear to be leading to a rural hotel," I whined in English.

"Rural lodgings rather than a hotel, as we don't want to be bothered with too much paperwork."

"That's a relief."

A while later she extracted a card from her purse and told me she intended to call Fede, the house-sourcing mechanic. Although I'd all but exhausted Don Andrés's list of cultural sights, I still had a few more vital attractions in reserve, so I persuaded her to wait a while, and after paying €16 apiece for the abundant fixed-price lunch, I asked her to show me the town's sports facilities.

"What on earth for?"

I puffed out my chest and tensed my stomach muscles. "Because I wish to continue my dynamic exercise regime and I want to know what my options are."

She smiled. "For some reason you're determined not to go back to the village today, aren't you?"

"I must finish my tour. We can drive over tomorrow morning," I said, praying that Don Andrés really was working behind the scenes.

"Muy bien. Vámonos."

Although I didn't really intend to use the athletics and cycling track or the other modern indoor and outdoor sports installations, I was as impressed by them as I was by the massive open-air pool which would be open from June. For such a small town in a comparatively poor part of Spain the facilities were marvellous. The friendly people were generally content with the health service, there were lots of cultural activities, no end of places to eat out, and there was little crime, so my initial impression was that Llerena had to be a superb place to live. Just then I saw no reason for us to elope to a boring village from where Mónica would have to commute to keep an eye on her parents. A modern house on the edge of town could be had for about €100,000, and as we wended our weary way home from a nearby nature reserve with a duckpond, I resolved to try to persuade her that our best bet might be to purchase one of those functional homes and live happily ever after without needing to worry about generating extra income.

All this, of course, would depend on the outcome of whatever Don Andrés was plotting.

"Brian, Brian, you're not going to believe this!" Mónica cried after rushing into my bedroom just before dinner time.

Freshly shaved and showered, I think the sanguine rush of blood to my cheeks went undetected.

"What's happened?"

"Tomorrow we're meeting Alberto and Lourdes in Almendralejo."

"To pick almonds?" I said with deliberate obtuseness, as I thought it crucial to show no knowledge of whatever it was that Don Andrés had arranged.

"No, silly, Almendralejo is a town not far from Mérida and a convenient place to meet up. Alberto has an appointment at the town hall in the morning, so we'll all meet at noon."

"That's great. So is it just a general get-together?"

"In principle, yes, but I *know* Alberto's got something important that he wants to talk about."

"Ah, good."

"In the end I emailed him about our rural tourism ideas, and when he called he was so excited that he was positively shouting down the phone."

"Oh. About that?"

"Not exactly. He's awfully eager to meet you, and he says Lourdes is too. We're going to try to convince her to come back here to live."

"Doesn't she like Cáceres then?"

"Well, she likes it well enough, but now that she's about to leave her stupid husband and their daughter's away in Madrid, what's to keep her there?"

"I don't know. Friends? The life she's made for herself?"

She flapped her hand. "Oh, what does that matter? Llerena's always been her real home, and she can do her work anywhere. Thank goodness she'll soon be free of that dreadful man."

"I take he wasn't very popular here."

"Daniel? Oh, he used to be a super guy, always the life and soul of our Christmas gatherings. Mamá had a real soft spot for him, because he always brought her a nice present and even accompanied her to church. Papá liked him too, because he'd bring him tobacco for the pipe he wasn't allowed to smoke but still did," she enthused.

"Er, your father referred to him as a cretinous chemist and a baboon."

"Ha, very funny. Daniel was… is very hirsute, and despite all his qualifications, rather dense."

After seating her beside me on the bed, I asked her to explain in simple terms how it was that the well-liked man's name had suddenly become mud.

She seemed perplexed. "That's obvious, isn't it?"

"Not to me."

"He's behaved very badly and Lourdes is going to leave him."

"Yes, I understand that, but he's still basically the same person, isn't he?"

She frowned. "Not to us, he isn't. Look, if he'd had a minor affair and it had all blown over, nobody would have minded much, because that's what men are like, but he's been meeting his latest tart openly, so that's the end of him as far as we're concerned." She chuckled. "I guess it's true that his minor defects have now become magnified in our eyes, but why shouldn't we deride him after what he's done to my sister?"

"I see. So if you caught me… and this is just an example… kissing Alicia in the kitchen, would I instantly become the most hateful person in the world?"

"Alicia has a moustache."

"Only a faint one."

She tittered. "Her lack of good looks is one reason Mamá employed her, because Papá's been known to be a bit naughty with the help, given half a chance, though he's past it now... I think."

"I see. So your father has probably... transgressed in his time, but you didn't all turn against him."

"Er, it's a bit different with blood relations, Brian. Edu wasn't always faithful to his poor wife Rosa, but all we could do was try to comfort her."

"Ah."

"And tell the oaf to be more discreet in future."

"OK, I think I'm beginning to get the picture. So, when I tire of you and begin to have affairs, as long as I keep them quiet, everything will be fine, is that it?"

"You, Brian?" She collapsed on the bed in a fit of laughter.

I made for the door. "I'm going to have my way with Alicia."

"Hoo, hoo, hoo! Good luck!"

This strong sense of family solidarity was brought home to me only five minutes later, because when Doña Luisa saw Mónica's moist, reddened eyes, she perused me grimly and sniffed, as if a passing skunk had taken a seat at her table.

"She has been laughing, Doña Luisa."

The lady grunted doubtfully.

"It's true, Mamá. I'm so pleased to be seeing Lourdes and Alberto tomorrow, and Brian is such a funny man, that I became almost hysterical with laughter."

Unwilling to be gawped at, and to show that I could also be devilish, I suddenly asked Doña Luisa what Lourdes's husband was like.

"Daniel? A wretched man living in mortal sin."

"So…"

But she cut me off with a loud tinkle of the bell.

"Oh, Mamá!" Mónica rushed out to intercept the cook.

While Doña Luisa was muttering a quick Our Father, I looked expectantly at her husband.

He smiled. "All roads lead to Almendralejo tomorrow, I believe, Brian."

"Yes, and, well… have you…?" I nodded encouragingly and even winked, I think.

"I've had a chat with my son and spelt things out to him, you know."

"Vale, gracias."

He raised his hands. "Now it's all in the lap of the gods."

"…into temptation, but deliver us from evil. Amen. And I've spoken to Lourdes. No matter what else you intend to talk about tomorrow, please try to convince that poor mistreated girl to come home."

I promised to do my best to lure (the forty-five-year-old) Lourdes back to Llerena.

11

Once I'd got used to driving the thirty-odd-year-old Citroen Dyane, I found that its 600cc engine hummed along nicely, rather like an oversized sewing machine on wheels. After a chilly start the bright sun soon raised the temperature to about fifteen degrees, so before reaching the dual carriageway near El Raposo I stopped to roll back the roof, eager to freshen up my brain cells before the potentially challenging encounter which lay before us. I was eager to meet two more of Mónica's siblings, but doubtful that trying to persuade Lourdes to return to Llerena was the right thing to do. From my point of view her presence could be beneficial, as it might divert Mónica's thoughts from this rural tourism scheme for a while, but to entice a grown woman away from the city where she'd lived for over twenty years, mainly to please her mother, seemed foolish to me.

It was Alberto who concerned me most, however, because I suspected that this well-connected man might hold the key to our future, so when the portly, besuited fellow strode out of the old town hall and hollered a greeting, I made ready to create a good first impression. After shaking my hand and squeezing my arm, he hugged and kissed his sister, asked after their parents and Cristina, then began to make it abundantly clear that he was extremely fond of the sound of his stentorian voice. Lourdes had been delayed by half an hour, so we killed some time in a nearby park, listening to his account of his move from sewage to tourism and scarcely getting a word in edgeways.

When the svelte figure of another stunning sister came striding towards us, Alberto bellowed joyfully and hurried off to embrace her.

"He's a great talker," I murmured to Mónica.

"Yes, he should be a politician, but bear with him, as he'll calm down once he begins to eat."

Lourdes's stylish clothes, glossy bobbed hair, and artfully applied makeup gave her the air of a film star, and her charming, easy manner made me believe that her husband must indeed be a cretinous baboon. Unlike her brother, she spoke softly and seemed curious about her sister's British beau, so while Alberto blathered on to Mónica, she and I lagged behind as we strolled to a nearby restaurant.

"I would like to read some of your articles, Lourdes," I said after she'd politely quizzed me for a while.

She wrinkled her divine little nose. "I'll send you some links, if you like, but it's mostly a lot of nonsense for the women's magazines. Recently I've been visiting some so-called celebrities in their ghastly homes and striving to write something positive about them, as that's what I'm paid for. What about you? Do you intend to do anything specific here, Brian?"

I told her briefly about Mónica's rural tourism crusade which had been gathering force ever since we'd arrived.

She chuckled. "Oh, she's always been an impetuous one. You ought to take your time and consider your options carefully."

"That's what everyone says, except her," I said boldly, sensing that I might have found a helpful ally.

As we entered the posh-looking eatery, still a few paces behind them, I asked her if she had any plans.

She smiled as she came to a halt on the marble steps. "At home I expect they've been speculating on my next move."

"Er, well, you have been discussed, yes."

She gazed at me. "Can you really see me living at home in Llerena?"

"Well…"

"Listening to my parents squabbling and jumping up whenever my mother rings her bell? No, you don't have to answer. The holidays are quite enough for me. Once we've sold our flat in Cáceres, I shall buy a nice apartment near the main square and go on with my pleasant life there."

"That sounds sensible."

She smiled. "I'm glad you think so."

"Hey, come on, you two!" Alberto yelled, so we soon sat down and he proceeded to order a whole host of tapas at the top of his voice.

Mónica had been right though, because no sooner had he stuck his fork into a slice of cured ham than he remained mostly silent, not because he ate like a glutton, but due to the way he intently savoured each mouthful of food and sip of costly red wine which the provincial government would be paying for. This welcome hiatus gave Mónica the chance to get to work on Lourdes, but it soon became apparent that her sister wasn't for moving, and her boyfriend was doing damn all to back up her far from convincing arguments.

"You like Llerena a lot, don't you, Brian?" was the last leading question she bothered to ask me, because I replied that although it suited an inquisitive but unadventurous foreigner like myself, a cosmopolitan university city like Cáceres had to be a livelier and less restricting place to live for a cultured lady like her sister.

Lourdes beamed, Mónica glowered, and by the time the seemingly endless succession of tapas finally ceased I was firmly in my best girl's bad books, though she had no opportunity to chide me, because the refuelled Alberto soon found his voice again. Fortunately he'd exhausted the sewage-tourism transition tale and what he had to say would soon consign my perfidy to oblivion.

"Papá told me what you wish to do, Mónica, and I've been giving it a great deal of thought," he said to us and the other dozen or so diners. "In sewage I could be of little help to my family and friends, it being a very specialised and generally unappealing line of work, but rural tourism has far more potential." He leant towards us and began to whisper loudly that since his chat with daddy he'd been exploring various avenues and believed that he would soon be able to create a job for his sister.

Mónica gasped. "What kind of job?"

He shrugged. "Well, give me a few ideas as to what you'd like to do, and I'll try my best to accommodate you."

"Can you really do that?" I asked.

He smiled smugly. "Why not? I'm not the top man – not yet, anyway – but I've already got so much dope on that old scoundrel that he'll be wise not to impede my... creativity."

"Still, a permanent post will surely have to be advertised," said Lourdes.

He grinned like a supercilious Siamese cat. "It'll be a temporary post, six months at a time, forever and ever, or until you tire of it or I move on to a new department. So, what do you say?"

"I... I... can I really create my own job?"

"Well, within reason, yes."

"You write just as well as I do," said Lourdes. "So perhaps you could sort of disseminate information about the area's attractions to the wider world."

"But how?"

"Oh, I have some useful contacts, and you could set up a website or just a simple blog about the area. Really there are no end of things you could write about."

"And you'll only be accountable to me," said Alberto. "So there'll be no pressure to speak of. The salary won't be especially generous, I'm afraid, as it'll be best not to make it a high-profile role." He sniggered complacently. "So just submit some kind of proposal and... oh, but there is one little issue that we ought to try to remedy. It's such a shame that wives don't adopt their husbands' surnames here as they do in other countries. Tell me, are you two thinking of getting married any time soon?"

I smiled. "I would love to marry your sister, but I believe we ought to wait for a while."

"Hmm, shame that. What are you surnames?"

"I only have one. It's Wilson, Brian Wilson, like the Beach Boy."

"Hmm, Wilson, yes, but of course if you marry here, Mónica will retain her family names. To give her a job might seem a bit like favoritism, you see."

"Yes, I can see that."

He kneaded his flabby cheeks for a while, then slapped the table. "I know! You can have the job, Brian, but it'll really be for the pair of you. How does that sound?"

Lourdes chuckled, Mónica scoffed, and I began to imitate a wide-mouthed fish out of water.

"You'll be our international tourism expert, you see. Did you get a degree?"

"Yes, in economics."

"That's perfect. We'll put the initials after your name and everyone'll be impressed. In Spain folk always think foreigners are cleverer than we are."

"I haven't even done any of the residence paperwork yet."

"Mónica will help you sort that out, won't you, dear?"

My sullen sweetheart sipped her water as she pondered on this. "Hmm, yes, but I'm not sure this ruse will work. Brian still needs to improve his spoken and written Castilian, and if I accompany him everywhere, what will people make of that? Besides, he doesn't have the kind of blustering self-confidence that enabled you to switch from sewage at the drop of a hat. In any sort of stressful situation with other people, I'm sure he'd become a nervous wreck and give the game away."

"Gracias," I said.

Alberto smiled. "But experts are notoriously poor public speakers, Mónica." He patted me lightly on the head. "Brian will be the brainbox behind all your schemes, while you'll be his public relations assistant, employed to steer the great tourism guru through the tiresome trials of daily life."

"So I'd be employed too, would I?"

"Well, I suppose you ought to be, but now we're back with the surname problem."

"This is getting out of hand," said Lourdes.

"Mucha imaginación," I said in impeccable Spanish.

Our prospective boss sighed. "Yes, we've got carried away."

Lourdes then suggested that the proposed post should be a low-profile one in which public appearances would play no part. We ought to simply go out and about to places of touristic interest, making notes and taking photos, then produce illustrated articles for an ostensibly independent blog which might or might not be read all over the world.

"That sounds good," I said.

"Yes, it does," my gradually thawing consort concurred.

"I can manage to pay you about… €1200 a month," said Alberto. "That oughtn't to raise too many eyebrows."

"And Brian Jones must be the employee," said M. "As you can't afford to risk a scandal over something like this."

Alberto laughed. "You're back in Spain now, little sister. What's one Beach Boy more or less in the provincial council?"

I smiled. "What will happen if Mónica and I fall out, Alberto?"

"Then I'll sack you on the spot."

"Vale."

After chatting about family matters for an hour or so, we parted company and hit the road, Alberto in his big, tax-payer-funded BMW, Lourdes in a nifty Toyota hybrid, and us in the bright green machine that our boss thought might look well in a few of our tourism photos, though Lourdes opined that the more classic 2CV, or a SEAT 600, would fit the bill better. As we whirred along the quiet dual-carriageway at about fifty miles an hour, I felt that a weight had been lifted from my buzzing mind. The modest salary which Alberto had proposed would provide us with a handy amount of disposable income, while my private pensions would easily cover our day-to-day costs, so once we'd each ransacked our savings to buy one of the newer houses on the edge of town, we'd be set up for life.

After relaying these upbeat thoughts to Mónica, I went on to say that our expenses-paid trips around Extremadura would be purely pleasurable affairs, because producing a few decent blog posts would be child's play between the two of us, considering how mediocre that type of literature usually was.

"Sí, Brian."

"Ha, I could write one for Llerena right away, if you like, then you can translate it."

"As you wish."

"Ah, yes, it's like a dream really. You know, Alberto talks a lot, but he's really helping us out and I appreciate that." I drummed my fingers on the slightly wobbly steering wheel and hummed a few bars of Good Vibrations. "Ha,

Brian Wilson, tourism guru. What a laugh! In reality I'll be your assistant, of course, and who knows? If we get into it and the blog takes off, we might make enough money from affiliate links and whatnot to retire from the provincial council, then you'll be able to sign the articles and take the credit you'll deserve," I babbled in increasingly broken Spanish.

She patted my thigh. "Yes, it all sounds really promising, and do you know the really great thing about this so-called job?"

"What's that, love?"

"That it'll hardly interfere with our rural lodging house at all."

I gripped the wheel and looked up at the darkening sky. Had there been a full moon, I might well have howled at it. Mónica did most of the talking during the rest of the drive.

12

"We've always been happy here," Juanjo said in the cosy sitting room of their modern terraced house, not far from the municipal swimming pool.

"And it's already paid for, so we have no more money worries," said Cristina, who'd agreed with me that due to the salary that Mónica and I would soon be receiving, it was sheer nonsense to get embroiled in the purchase of a scruffy old house that we'd need to do up, before opening its doors to complete strangers who probably wouldn't come in sufficient numbers to make it worthwhile anyway.

It was Friday evening, our first away from the family home, and I was thoroughly enjoying our quiet dinner with the contented couple. At home there was never a moment's peace, as Don Andrés would act the goat until Doña Luisa reached for her bell or her beads, and the enjoyment I got from these lively meals was already wearing a bit thin. The conversation usually revolved around one or more of their children, and though eager to hear all about them, I was beginning to feel like a mere appendage to the extended family, rather than a worthwhile individual in my own right. It was better than spending almost every evening alone in Lancaster, but I really wanted us to begin to lay the groundwork for our future independence.

Don Andrés had told me that while his wife wouldn't approve of us living in sin, she knew it was the way of the heathenish modern world and would probably prefer that to a hasty marriage, because she was yet to be convinced that I was the right man for her daughter. Although she believed me to be a fine, upstanding chap – and my lapsed Protestantism didn't distress her too much, as at least we embraced the teachings of the Lord Jesus – she didn't seem to see foreigners as fully three-dimensional people.

As children growing up in the fifties, he explained, at school they'd been taught that God-fearing Spaniards were superior to folk from other lands. Although it was very kind of those funny Americans to pump billions of pesetas into the Spanish economy, one had to be wary of their heinous influence, or they'd end up polluting Spain's pure Catholic youth with their wanton ways. For the likes of his wife, even Spain's entry into the EEC in 1986 had been a double-edged sword, as although she saw with her own eyes the vast improvements to the roads and other infrastructure which followed, she feared that consorting with so many foreign nations would make her already corrupted country even worse.

As a result of Doña Luisa's somewhat condescending attitude towards me, I felt even more determined to fly the nest as soon as we were able. Although Mónica and I had already had the odd little tiff, invariably due to my disobedience, she was pleased and relieved by how well I was adapting to my new life, having feared that their domestic shenanigans might cause my morale to crumble or even send me racing to the airport.

In short, by then I was feeling on solid enough ground to wish to purchase something solid above me, namely a sensible house like Juanjo and Cristina's, or even a slightly better one, like brother Edu's modern detached place near the bullring/auditorium. Ever practical, I believed that even if our relationship failed to prosper, a half share in a contemporary dwelling in a thriving little town would be money well-spent, but how to convince Mónica to shelve her tiresome scheme, at least for a year or two?

At Juanjo and Cristina's it was a house rule never to speak of her family during meals, but our forthcoming job, although undeniably a family affair, was discussed at length. Juanjo pointed out that although Extremadura was full of touristic marvels, it was a shame that many of the best ones lay outside the boundaries of the Province of Badajoz. He opined that the real provincial jewel was Mérida, and while Badajoz had its splendid Alcazaba, a twelfth-century Moorish citadel with extensive gardens, as well as other lesser monuments, it was a bit of a grim city on the whole, the fine old centre being surrounded by endless blocks of soulless flats.

"Zafra and Jerez de los Caballeros are definitely worth visiting, and of course Llerena itself is one of the wonders of the world, but other than those places... well, I guess there are a few nice villages, and lots of good hunting country."

"Hiking country for *our* tourists," Mónica said, before gazing sadly at a large photo of Juanjo and his pals standing over a bloody, thoroughly dead wild boar.

"Yes, well, each to his own, but the point is that if Alberto will let you expand your horizons a bit, you'll be able to venture up to Cáceres, Trujillo and Guadalupe, all super-famous places."

Mónica looked at me. "Lourdes could write us a lovely piece about Cáceres in no time. Trujillo, with its awesome medieval and renaissance buildings, already receives thousands of tourists from all over the world, and I doubt we'd have anything new to say about it. Guadalupe too, with its fabulous monastery, is a long-established destination and a Unesco site."

"I'd like to go to those places."

"And we will, but for our work I believe we ought to stay within our province, to please our boss. I've even begun to think that as literature about Mérida abounds – though I could soon rattle off an article if my brother wants one – we should first do Zafra and Jerez de los Caballeros, then concentrate wholly on the Campiña Sur."

Cristina frowned. "But what the heck is there worth seeing here, apart from this place?"

"Lots of things that the curious tourist is just waiting to discover. Interesting villages like Azuaga and Berlanga, La Jayona mine, the Mudéjar hermitage of the Virgen del Ara, the Alcazaba de Reina and, above all, our Roman city of Regina."

"City?" I muttered.

Juanjo smiled. "You've been doing your homework."

Cristina snorted. "If I came from Madrid or even abroad, I wouldn't want to be bothering with those piddling little places. The Campiña Sur must be just about the most boring part of Extremadura."

"Plasencia's worse," said Juanjo.

"Plasencia's medieval quarter is beautiful," said M.

"Yes, well, I bought a couple of really duff cars up there."

Mónica raised her hands and let them fall, a bit like Mussolini (or that poor imitation, Franco) striving to grab the crowd's attention. "I've been giving this a lot of thought and I've reached the conclusion that if Brian and I wish to do something truly original and useful in our work, we'll be better off concentrating on these lesser-known places which are closer to home. After all, typical tourists will see all the famous sights on their first visit to Extremadura, so before they return we must show them where to find the hidden gems of our region."

"I'd just go somewhere else, myself," said Juanjo. "Like Las Vegas."

Mónica smiled. "There are places for every taste. I imagine our visitors to be curious, contemplative people who eschew the crowds in favour of tranquillity, fresh air, healthy pursuits, and the odd cultural outing from time to time."

"You sound like a tourist brochure," said Cristina.

"Well, I suppose my mind is already on our work. Our tourists will come to the Campiña Sur to pursue a programme of active relaxation. They'll prefer to stay in a comfortable place which makes them feel at one with their surroundings, rather than a bustling hotel. They'll wish to step out of their accommodation to engage with the local people, or simply head off for an invigorating walk in the hills or through the fields."

My eyes narrowed, because I'd realised exactly where she wished *our* tourists to stay. I'd also twigged that she meant to tailor the articles we'd soon be writing to her own ends. Our tourists, after each day spent exploring the Campiña Sur, would retire to *our* lodging house, presumably in Casas de Reina, or maybe Reina, another small village only two more miles down the road.

As it would soon be time to leave, I decided not to reveal her intentions to the others, because the tipsy Cristina might mock her proposal in no uncertain terms and reveal that I too was still sceptical about the idea. That week I'd been biding my time, you see, hoping that Mónica would come around to my way of thinking. I'd heard no more about Fede the tractor mechanic and we'd already begun to do some research for our articles. I'd hoped that our pleasant dinner at her sister's cosy home might tip the balance and make her more amenable to buying a similar dwelling, but I now saw that I'd underestimated her. Still, a softly-softly approach was preferable to a heated debate, so I bided my time until we'd begun to walk home, before observing that she still seemed set on her rural lodging house.

She took my hand and smiled. "Yes, but don't worry. I've realised that it's asking too much of you to participate in such a venture at this early stage."

"Right, so will we wait for a while?"

"I'm not sure. Fede's going to show me some houses on Sunday morning, when he's free from the job which I've checked that he does actually have. The properties he has in mind aren't officially for sale. Those that are can only be viewed with an estate agent. I'll be seeing houses which belong to his family and friends, houses they've been reluctant to sell in case their faraway relatives decide to come home one day. As time passes, however, and those relatives remain in the cities or abroad, the houses fall into disrepair and the desire to get rid of them grows. I gather that Fede has a stake in two of them, so he'll undoubtedly try to sell me one of those, but I shan't be making any snap decisions, as if I drag my heels the price is sure to come down."

"I see." I pictured the handsome young chap. "So have you been seeing this Fede behind my back?" I said lightly.

She tittered. "Only speaking to him behind your back. I needed to find out what motivated him, and now I believe I know." She squeezed my hand. "I don't intend to spend more than sixty or seventy thousand, as I can spare a hundred altogether and I'll need some money to have it done up."

She hadn't referred to herself in the first person singular so much since the day we'd met, and due to our united front concerning most matters, I found it unsettling. It might just be a ruse to force my hand, but that would hardly be

Mónica's style, as she'd always been transparent with me, I mused, wondering what to say.

"You must remember, Brian, that I've had the idea of setting up some kind of tourism-related business for a long time, and deep down I think I knew it would be something straightforward like this. I even thought about doing it instead of going abroad to work, but I decided that a clean break was best after my marriage ended. In Manchester I was able to view my options more objectively, and the more money I saved, the more eager I became. Then you came along and I suppose I just assumed that you'd be up for something that so many of your compatriots like to do, but I see now that I was wrong."

We'd reached the main square by this time and, by accident or design, Mónica came to a halt by the bronze statue of Zurbarán. With his brush hand extended and a benign expression on his bearded face, he appeared to be surveying the square for a suitable subject to paint. Would he choose me, I wondered, with my placid face, the faint lines upon it etched by years of cautious living, or Mónica, who was gazing fearlessly into the future, eager to do something with the latter part of her life, rather than bumbling comfortably along as I wished to do?

"The thing is, Brian, to buy a house in town just to live in it seems like an awfully dull thing to do. We can easily do that when we're old, but now we're in the prime of life, so I feel we ought to be less cautious and buy a place with possibilities."

"I believe you're reading my thoughts."

"Hmm, let's just go to see these houses with an open mind, shall we?"

"Mine or yours?" I quipped.

She took my arm. "I'd like us to wish for the same thing, so I don't want you to worry too much about those tourists of mine." She chuckled. "I do get carried away sometimes, but this house I'd like us to buy will be principally for us. We may end up having paying guests from time to time, or our lives might take another direction entirely. This job that Alberto's going to give us may lead to better ideas which we'll wish to put into practice."

"Such as what?"

She sighed. "I really don't know. We may end up keeping goats, or providing... camel rides, or growing vegetables, or writing books, or any number of other things."

My mind produced a vivid image of a camel poking its head through a kitchen window.

"It doesn't really matter what we end up doing, Brian, but we have to do something. It's the journey rather than the destination that's important."

"Hmm."

"Don't you agree?"

I looked at Francisco de Z. and he appeared to give the nod to the tremendously reckless thing that I'd suddenly decided to do.

"Brian?"

After all, polar explorers of yore had fearlessly set out, unsure if they'd ever return, while even now elderly Indians renounced their worldly possessions and took to the road, living from hand to mouth and discovering their spiritual selves…

"Are you angry?"

Folk travelled around the world by bicycle, or scaled rock faces without ropes, and the odd impecunious poet might still be starving in his garret, so why couldn't I also throw caution to the wind and expose myself to the slings and arrows of outrageous fortune for once in my life?

"Oh, you're sulking."

I turned to face her with a steely glint in my eyes, I hoped.

"Mónica."

"Sí?"

I thrust back my shoulders. "Mónica, I have just made an important, life-changing decision that will demonstrate my commitment to our new life."

"What is it?"

I rubbed my chilly hands together, then patted her rosy cheeks. "This will prove once and for all that I'm not some hyper-cautious… former furniture salesman who has no sense of adventure."

"Well?"

I wagged a finger at her. "And don't think that because I've had a few glasses of wine that I'll go back on my word in the clear light of day, because my mind is made up and nothing or no-one can make me change it."

"Tell me then."

"I'm going to… sell my house."

She smiled. "Yes, I was going to suggest that you ought to do that."

"Oh."

She took my hands. "You've survived a week, after all, so if you still love me as I love you, you might as well throw in your lot with me."

I gulped, reluctant to tell her that I wished to use some of the proceeds to buy a sensible town house – as an investment, if nothing else – because that would have spoilt the effect.

"Yes, love, that's just what I want to do."

As we kissed I thought I saw Zurbarán's right hand move.

13

On Saturday morning I awoke with cold feet, and not only because the duvet was up around my knees. My house in Lancaster would soon have tenants and I'd be coining it in, and besides, what would my son and heir think about me effectively severing my material ties with good old Blighty so soon? After another combative breakfast, caused by Don Andrés farting when his wife was saying grace, I repaired to the big sitting room to give Ben a video call.

I'd chosen that room in order to show my son that I'd landed on my feet among landed gentry, and he wasn't to know that it was freezing cold in there and would remain so all day, unless Don Andrés was ejected from the parlour and had to light a fire. After I'd shown Ben the portraits of Mónica's great-great-great-grandparents, he wished to meet her living relatives, so I reluctantly entered the parlour and pointed the camera at the still bickering couple.

Although Ben was familiar with the formal 'usted' form, he refused to use it as a matter of principle, believing all people to be equal, so it was amusing to see Doña Luisa cringe when he addressed her in a most familiar manner and said that he hoped his boring old dad was behaving himself.

"Your father is a very considerate guest," she said coolly.

Don Andrés enjoyed Ben's faux pas even more than I did, then attempted to embarrass him by asking if he'd had many women lately.

"Oh, five or six so far this year. How about you, Andrés?"

"Ah, unfortunately my gout and before that my stomach ulcer have stopped me from getting out much, but now that I'm relatively healthy, I expect I'll soon be shagging the local wenches again."

"Andrés!" Doña Luisa cried.

"As well as my eight official children, I also have several bastards out there, conceived during my spell of military service, so you have a lot of catching up to do, my lad."

Ben laughed. "I'll do my best." He smiled at the fuming lady. "Sorry about that, Luisa."

She winced pleasantly. "My husband is an appalling influence and I hope that when you come to visit at Christmas you'll choose to spend your time with the more civilised people who occasionally inhabit this house."

"Will do, Luisa. Where's Mónica?"

"In the kitchen, where she belongs," I said, but as usual *my* wisecrack didn't go down too well, probably due to my excessively deadpan delivery.

Ben wished to speak to her alone, so after handing her the phone I returned to the parlour and apologised to Doña L. for my son's informality and crude allusion to promiscuity.

She sighed. "By now I'm used to the youth of today, having so many grandchildren. One must make allowances, as the world that I grew up in has vanished forever."

"Thank God," said her husband.

She smiled. "Your son is a charming, spirited young man and I'm looking forward to seeing him at Christmastime."

"I'm glad, Doña Luisa," I said, wondering if Ben had inherited his charm from his mother, because at his age I'd been neither a success with the ladies nor a renowned wit. His sterner side was also more effective than mine, so when Mónica returned my phone and he ordered me into the other room, I meekly complied.

"Bloody hell, Dad. Why are you so down on Mónica's brilliant scheme?"

"I'm not down on it, merely cautious. We oughtn't to rush into anything just yet, and the job I'm sure she's told you about should keep us occupied throughout the winter."

"Balls. That sounds more like charity than a job. Talk about nepotism! You ought to be ashamed of yourselves for agreeing to waste the poor taxpayers' money like that. Besides, it'll either never happen or not last for long, so if I were you I'd tell her bro' thanks but no thanks."

I was astonished by his radical point of view, as everyone else had thought that landing this nice little earner was a great piece of luck, and what was family for, after all?

"Yes, you might well gawp at me, Dad. Christ, with your pensions and all the money you'll have after selling your house, why do you need to go scratting around for even more cash?"

I raised my chin. "I'll have you know that Mónica is extremely keen to… for us to take the job seriously and produce some top-notch material to draw tourists to this neglected corner of Spain."

"Yeah, she said, but reading between her lines I can tell that she knows deep down that it's a pretty contemptible way to go about it."

I snorted like an offended thoroughbred. "Tell me, Ben, where did you develop this penetrating insight into Spanish ways, and why might the job never happen or not last for long?"

"Last year I lived in Zaragoza for four months, remember. I made a couple of good friends and got the lowdown on what makes Spain tick. I heard plenty of stories about favouritism and there are always winners and losers, like the folk who think they've passed a state exam to get a good job, then suddenly find themselves further down the list, because some bastard's slipped a few new names onto it, in return for a juicy backhander somewhere down the line."

"But Alberto is just–"

"Yeah, and that brother sounds like a right schemer, shifting from sewage to tourism just like that. And don't forget that if you do take this crappy job, you'll be forever in his debt, and who's to say he won't call in a favour one day that might land you both in the shit?"

I snorted like a weary donkey. "This is all very Machiavellian, Ben, and my battery's running low."

"Hmm, well, I guess that job's no big deal, not compared to you putting the brakes on Mónica's awesome plan."

"Twelve percent."

"Eh?"

"The battery."

"Right, listen up. Forget about buying a boring house in town, as you won't need to live there till you're old and knackered. As for your place in Lancaster, call the rental agency right away and tell them you've changed your mind, then contact an estate agent's and get them to flog it."

"But most of my things are still–"

"I'll get your important stuff shifted to mum's house for now, and I'll sell or donate the furniture."

Recalling the detached house with a large attic and double garage which I used to co-own, I agreed that this might be a good plan.

"Course it is. So, that'll be this end sorted, and I won't charge you a penny for my services."

I smiled. "If I decide to sell, you may keep whatever you get for the furniture, which won't be a lot, but you must store my books somewhere dry."

"Will do. Now, you've got to go to see those village houses tomorrow in a positive frame of mind. Having said that, I reckon that Mónica might be ruled by her heart, so you're going to have to use your head and make sure you don't end up with some great rambling money pit that'll take an age to do up."

"We won't, because I really don't want to stay here for longer than I have to," I murmured.

"Oh, you're right as rain there, Dad. Just think how lucky you are to be slap bang in the bosom of an old Spanish family. Some folk would give their right arm to be in your shoes."

"Yes, but…"

"Ha, it's like a crash course in integration that you're getting, unlike all those poor mutts who live on the coast for twenty years and never step inside a local's home. I know living there's not perfect, but when you do move out, you'll look back on your time there fondly, I bet."

"Maybe. Nine percent."

"You could plug it in, but I'm nearly done. If you do see a house that you like tomorrow, make sure you deal with the owner face to face. It's fair enough for this tractor guy to get a little cut, but I've heard horror stories about agents whacking thirty or forty grand on the price, then somehow keeping it for themselves, so keep your wits about you."

"Yes, I will. I must say, Ben, that for a twenty-two-year-old you do show remarkable maturity when it suits you. I'm sure you'll go far after you graduate next summer."

"Yeah? Where do you see me going?"

"Oh, to some big company in London, Madrid or Paris, I expect."

"Not on your life, dude. There'll be no bloody rat race and decades of drudgery for me, I can tell you that now. As soon as I finish – and don't bother coming to the graduation, 'cause I won't be there – I'll be off on a tour of Spain, seeing what's what and where I can make a living. I expect I'll land at your *village* house at some point, so make sure there's a spare room for me, eh?"

"Yes, Ben. Four percent."

"That's all I have to say for now, but I'll be calling Mónica tomorrow aft and woe betide if you've been following her round like a wet dishcloth, putting the dampers on her dream."

I pictured a wet dishcloth with legs and, funnily enough, a camel's head.

"I can't take any more advice now, Ben. I've begun to have surreal visions. Two percent."

"Good luck!"

Beep, beep, beep.

I trudged into the parlour and slumped into an armchair.

Don Andrés grinned. "All good, Brian?"

"I think so."

He leant over and ruffled my remaining hair. "Don't worry about a thing, because I'm coming with you tomorrow."

"Ah, good."

"Papá knows how to deal with village people."

Doña Luisa crossed herself.

14

On that cold, cloudy Sunday morning Fede the mechanic showed us around four houses, but I'm going to cut to the chase and only tell you about the last one. After seeing a great rambling money pit in the village of Reina, and two uninspiring properties in Casas de Reina, Fede led us past the big old church and along a narrow street to a dwelling that belonged to his aunt, he said, who had lived in Zaragoza for the last twenty-odd years, since her marriage to a Llerenense who had become a fireman in the sprawling capital of Aragón.

Don Andrés, wearing his usual tweed suit, had chattered excitedly during the drive there in the Dyane, but after greeting Fede he'd remained stonily silent as he followed us around, wielding the stick that he no longer needed and scowling at everything he saw. He now asked our guide in which neighbourhood of Zaragoza his aunt lived.

"In El Rabal, not far from the river."

"A nice area." He winked at me. "I know most of Spain from my machinery-selling days."

With the true ownership of the property verified in Don Andrés's eyes, we viewed the long, off-white, two-storey corner house which seemed to be somewhat lacking in windows. I mentioned this.

"Most of the rooms have only one window," said Fede. "When it was built in the nineteenth century, having abundant light wasn't considered important. Although the first owner was probably quite well off, his priority would have been to keep out the winter cold and the summer heat," said the articulate mechanic. "You could put in more windows, of course, but the walls are very thick, so it might prove to be an expensive job. Do you want to see inside?"

"Sí," Mónica said eagerly, earning herself a jab in the back from her father.

"We might as well," I said with a shrug, before feigning such an unconvincing a yawn that Fede sniggered as he unlocked the big old door.

Having expected to find the place in a state of disrepair, I was surprised to enter a large, blue-and-white-tiled lobby with a couple of upright chairs, some old paintings, and a narrow table with a few tacky ornaments on it.

"It's very dusty," I said to conceal the generally positive feeling I had, as the room which Fede and Mónica were making for appeared to contain a full complement of furniture.

On attempting to follow them, I found Don Andrés's stick barring my way.

"Stay here, you. The last thing we need is a damned foreigner messing things up."

I bridled like an insulted stallion. "*My* money will be buying this or some other place too, you know."

"Yes, that's the trouble. Look, this Fede's no bumpkin, but I bet he still believes that you guiris (an uncomplimentary word for foreigner) are made of money. He'll realise, of course, that my daughter and I are superior people, due to our dignified bearing and polished speech, but coming in that ugly old Citroen was a stroke of genius, because he'll believe that like so many other noble folk, we've been reduced to penury."

"I doubt it."

"Oh, he will once I've got to work on him. That's why I've quelled my habitual urge to talk and instead cultivated a brooding, slightly pitiful presence. Do you follow me?"

"Er, not really."

"I told Mónica not to jabber too much either. If she likes this old place, and you do too, she'll give me the nod and I'll spring into action."

I gulped. "How, exactly?"

He grabbed the lapel of my thick walking jacket and eyeballed me. "I'll say that the place is really for me, her widowed father who's had to sell the old family home and needs to find a fitting place in which to live out his remaining years. Once I've told him all about my fine pedigree, he'll understand that a man of my station couldn't possibly live in some poky flat. Despite the evils of the modern world and the ravages of socialism, these peasants still look up to us, so once he's heard my sob story, I'm sure he'll tell that aunt of his to lower the price a bit. Right, let's go and see what's what."

I barred his way with my mighty right arm, now capable of doing thirty press-ups, with the help of the other one, of course.

"Let me go! Didn't you hear Mónica's delighted chirrup? If I don't act fast, he'll be adding twenty thousand to the price."

"Andrés, don't be absurd. How could we live in a small village like this after you'd told such a pack of lies? We'd be… pariahs from the word go, so forget all that nonsense and go on keeping your mouth shut, por favor."

He growled softly and grinned, but to this day I don't know just how serious he'd been about telling that cock and bull story.

"All right, but you stay out of their way too, because he'll see euro signs in those naive blue eyes of yours."

"Pound signs," I corrected, but we did go off to explore the rooms alone, trusting Mónica not to show too much enthusiasm if she liked what she saw.

In a way the ground floor – comprising a large kitchen, a spacious sitting room, a cosy parlour, a smallish bedroom, a utility room, and a tiny bathroom – looked like a Spanish film set from the fifties or sixties which had been frozen in time and dust. After mentally stripping away the ugly lampshades, religious pictures, horrendous ornaments and so on, I saw that after a thorough dusting and mopping, most of the rooms wouldn't look too bad at all. The paint was a bit flaky in places, but I saw no damp patches, and my heart leapt when I recalled that wallpaper – the lazy DIYer's nightmare – was almost unheard of in Spain. The tiled floors crackled in places, but a few dollops of cement and a spot of grouting would sort them out, and the windows, although single-glazed, seemed solid enough.

"Could you live here, Andrés?" I asked him in the sitting room whose shabby sofa and armchairs would have to go, whereas the solid dinner table and six chairs looked good for another few generations.

He smiled. "Is that an invitation?"

"No… I mean, yes, but not to live, unless Doña Luisa finally throws you out."

"Ah, the poor woman would pine away without me to nag all day long. In answer to your question, yes, a stoical fellow like me – and you too, no doubt – could live here perfectly well, but the burning question now is whether my daughter would be happy to make a few improvements to a fine old place like this, or if she'd wish to strip it from floor to roof and start afresh."

I sighed. "Yes, that's the million-dollar question."

He asked me if she'd given me any indication as to the likelihood of her wishing to transform a property or just tart it up a bit.

"It isn't something we've discussed much. What do you think she'll want to do?"

"It's hard to say," he said, before reviewing his other daughters' attitudes to that kind of thing. Mari Carmen in Madrid, a part-time music teacher who was married to a bank manager, had spent a fortune renovating an enormous old flat in the Barrio de las Letras, a neighbourhood once home to seventeenth-century literary luminaries such as Lope de

Vega, Quevedo and the great Cervantes, although Don Andrés believed that many of the buildings had been replaced at a later date. Cristina, on the other hand, had plumped for her modern house, and Lourdes's spacious flat in Cáceres had been modernised before they'd bought it.

"And as for the boys, well, only Felipe in Salamanca lives in a really old flat, but he doesn't earn much as an architect's assistant, having failed to complete his degree, so as far as I know, he and his dozy wife haven't done much to it."

By this time Fede and Mónica seemed to be directly overhead, so I suggested that we go up to join them.

He cupped his ear and frowned. "More chirruping, the silly girl. Given her failure to dissimulate her delight, we'll be as well to go outside and take a peek at what really matters."

"All right."

After inspecting the spacious, scruffy rear patio, we walked back through the house to the street. I pointed out that a bit rendering and a fresh coat of whitewash would make the walls look great.

"It isn't the walls that worry me, Brian, as they're at least half a metre thick. Damn it, this street's too narrow to see." He rapped on the door of the house opposite and an elderly lady soon opened it. "Señora, would you be kind enough to allow us inside to peruse the roof of the house opposite which my daughter and son-in-law may wish to purchase?"

Due to his peremptory tone I feared she might tell us to take a hike, but she happily ushered us inside and treated the old rogue with a degree of deference that surprised me. To me Don Andrés, though a thoroughly likeable man, seemed more clownish than dignified, but his reception appeared to show that old attitudes still lingered among people of a certain age.

From a bedroom window we saw that at least the visible half of the roof was in good condition, with the curved, reddish tiles all in their place and the cement we could see not looking too crumbly. It transpired that Fede's great-uncle had sold his little remaining land to thoroughly renovate the roof about thirty years earlier, hoping that it would encourage his only daughter to stick around, but he hadn't counted on a son-in-law who valued a job for life more than his roots.

"So, after her parents died, Reme came home from Zaragoza less often, and in recent years she's hardly been at all, what with her little grandchildren and all."

"Ah, that's the way of the world these days," said Don A.

"Sí, señor, it certainly is."

"So is Reme doing well up there in the north?"

"Oh, yes, I believe so. Those that leave always seem to do all right for themselves. Does the foreign gentleman not understand Castilian?"

"I…" I felt the end of a walking stick on my foot.

"Ah, my dear son-in-law is a man of few words, and he's been suffering from… tuberculosis."

The lady stepped back.

"Oh, he's cured now, but his doctor has insisted that he must live in the country, preferably in a place with cold and fairly dry winters."

"He's come to the right place then. We're very high up here and it can get awfully cold at night." She smiled at me sympathetically. "You must sleep well wrapped up with a window open, young man," she said slowly. "Then those poor lungs of yours will be as good as new in no time."

I cleared my throat. "Yes, I'll do that."

"Ooh, he's looking a bit feverish."

Don Andrés knew that his absurd statement had sent a rush of blood to my cheeks, but he wasn't done yet.

"Yes, although cured of the disease, his convalescence will be a lengthy one. My daughter has given up her job in order to nurse him, so they'll be in straitened circumstances for some time." He looked over at the house and sighed. "I only hope that Fede's aunt isn't asking too much for the old place."

The lady folded her arms and smiled. "I believe that over the years the price has come down from a hundred to ninety to eighty, and maybe even less by now. Nobody wants to move here, you see, despite old Agustín harping on about our Roman theatre and whatnot."

"Who is Agustín?" I said weakly, the psychosomatic effects of Don Andrés's porker having already kicked in.

"The mayor. We elected him after he retired and came back to live here, because he's an educated man. He seems to think that our historical patrimony, as he calls it, will bring folk in droves, to visit or even to live, but I can't see how a pile of Roman stones is going to put food on anyone's plate. I mean, can you?"

"Indeed not, señora. I'd say that young Fede's aunt will be jolly lucky to sell the place at all, things being the way they are."

She sighed. "That's what I said to my Juan, before he died the year before last." She crossed herself.

"I'm sorry to hear that. Ah, I suppose you'd like to have neighbours across the street, instead of a big empty house."

"Well, we all look out for each other here and I don't get too lonely, but yes, it is a shame to step out every day to see the old place with no plant pots like there used to be."

"Ah, and no cheery greeting either. An empty house is indeed a sad thing to behold. My son-in-law..." He noticed my forbidding frown. "...that's to say, my daughter is a keen horticulturalist, so if they can afford to buy the place, I'm sure you'll see flowers blooming away from spring to autumn, won't she, Brian?"

"Sí," I hissed, but on seeing the lady's beaming face I followed up with a few more friendly words.

Don Andrés patted me softly on the back for my effort, before asking her if she kept in touch with her old friend Reme.

"Oh, she calls me now and then, normally about the house. A few people have been to see it over the years, but they must not have liked it, or the price. I'll certainly be having a word with her about your visit."

The old scoundrel turned to wink at me, then pointed across the way. "Look at my daughter, gabbing away to young Fede. Ah, I only hope that her dream of an affordable village house will come true, then I'll be able to live out my remaining days contentedly, knowing that all twelve of my children and their spouses are settled."

"Oh, twelve children!"

Fearing another fictitious outpouring, I steered him towards the stairs and we'd soon taken our leave of the amiable old lady who I strongly suspected would soon be my neighbour. Out on the street I only had time to call him a silly old goat before he entered the house and hurried up the stairs at great speed for a man who'd almost died of gout a few weeks earlier. Fede met us on the landing and just behind him I was shocked to see Mónica holding an unfamiliar bunch of keys.

Fede smiled. "Don't worry, Brian. I'm off to the bar to let you discuss the house in peace. I'll await you there." He trotted down the stairs and we soon heard the thud of the door.

I could see that Mónica was striving to contain her feeling of glee, knowing that she still had to convince her tough, no-nonsense boyfriend that this was the place for us. Saying barely a word, she showed us the two quaintly furnished bedrooms and an antiquated bathroom, before opening a secure door to a large, untiled space with a single window at the end, close to a metal door opening onto some steps down to the patio.

"This, for me, is a crucial part of the house."

I scuffed my shoe on the concrete floor and sniggered nervously. "It looks like a huge prison cell right now." I gazed around at the three blank, whitewashed walls. "This explains the shortage of windows."

"This space would have been used for storing the wheat and whatnot," said Don Andrés.

"Yes, it'll be handy for storage," I said hopefully.

"What do you both think of the rest of the house?"

"It's a grand old place with a solid roof," said her father.

"With a bit of renovation and a few new items of furniture, I think it'll be just fine," I said with my fingers crossed behind my back.

When she agreed, I made a fist of that hand and squeezed with relief. Thank goodness she didn't wish to spend a fortune on a full refurbishment and thus turn what seemed like a moderately priced house into a gaping money pit.

"We'd be able to smarten up the main house ourselves, without spending too much money, although I would want white bathroom suites eventually."

"Of course, love." I recalled a worrying word she'd uttered. "Er, what do you mean by the *main* house?"

She made a sweeping gesture around the former storeroom. "This would be our independent guest quarters." She began to pace around. "They'd come up those steps into a living area with a kitchenette. Here would be the bedroom, which would need a window, and there the bathroom, which can do without one, I think."

Don Andrés hooted with laughter and slapped the wall. "You'd better get yourself a pickaxe, Brian. Oh, boy, for a man recovering from a grave illness, you're going to have your work cut out to install that window."

I explained to my startled sweetheart what her father had said to the nice lady neighbour.

She shrugged. "That's all right. We'll just tell her he's a senile old fool."

"Ha ha, but not just yet, my dear, because said neighbour is going to put in a good word for you with the owner. I shouldn't be surprised if my foolishness saves you ten thousand or so."

"I've already told Fede what we might be willing to pay. Anyway, Brian won't need a pickaxe, because real builders will do… would do this job, once we'd got whatever permission is required." She took my limp left hand and squeezed it. "But I'd be in no hurry to begin. We'd settle in first and make sure we liked living here, don't you think?"

"Well, yes, if this is what you want."

She smiled. "That depends on you too, and the price, of course. I've told him we might be willing to pay seventy-five thousand, five less than the asking price."

On trying to recall my precise feelings at that moment in time, it all seems like a bit of a blur. The big old place didn't thrill me as it did Mónica, but it seemed remarkably good value for money and I liked the look of the village. If we didn't buy that one, we'd surely end up somewhere similar anyway, and the solid roof, fortress-like walls, lack of damp, and suitability for my partner's pet project made me disregard my minor pangs of anxiety and tell her that in principle I was up for it.

"Oh, Brian!" she hugged me.

"Pending a thorough survey," I wheezed.

"Bah, survey!" Don Andrés cried, before pointing at a hatch in the ceiling. "Find me some stepladders and I'll do one right now."

So the two of us trooped back to the neighbour's house and soon returned with some ladders and a torch to inspect the underside of the roof. On seeing several newish beams and barely a chink of light through the tiles, Don Andrés clambered down and declared the survey complete.

"You won't find a better roof for miles around."

"Er, I'd still like to have the whole house surveyed."

"As you wish, but a man who cares for his roof, cares for the rest of his house too."

Just then, with the switched off torch in my hand, an inner light must have illuminated my face, because something had occurred to me that made the whole business seem far more appealing. Mónica had won me over, that was true, but until my brainwave I'd foreseen weeks or even months of hanging around, waiting for the sale to go through, followed by a spring and summer dedicated to dratted DIY tasks. Fede seemed like an easy-going bloke, and I suspected his aunt would be fairly laid back too, judging by the way she'd left the family home unattended for so long…

Mónica nudged me. "Have you suddenly realised what a wonderful house it is, Brian?"

"Eh? Oh, yes. Let's join Fede in the bar."

She beamed and made to leave, only to find her father barring her way with his stick.

"Not so fast, young lady. I strongly advise against too much fraternisation at this point in proceedings. If I were you I'd step into the bar, confirm your offer for the house, hand over the keys, and bid him good day."

"That would seem impolite."

"Look, if you go in there chirruping away, he'll tell his aunt that you're in love with her blasted house and she'll get another five thousand out of you."

"We'll have a quick coffee," I said decisively. "And not chirrup at all."

"Muy bien, have it your way."

The bar was in fact the restaurant where we'd had lunch the previous Sunday. Fede assured us that the youngish owners, María José and José Ángel, encouraged the villagers to pop in for a drink whenever they wished, just as they had before the place had become a popular eatery due to the influx of trippers in recent years. Much as I'd have liked to chew the fat with the pleasant young fellow who actually lived in Llerena, I wished to ascertain just one thing before heading back to town.

"Fede, if we do end up buying the house, will we be able to begin to do some work on it before the sale is concluded."

"I don't see why not, Brian. Will you be getting a mortgage?"

"No."

"Then there should be no complications. My aunt will want the entire payment to be official, without the cash amount that some sellers insist on to pay less tax, so as soon as the preliminary contract has been drawn up, I don't think she'll mind you having the keys and getting started. I'll ask her when I tell her your offer and let you know soon."

Due to his aunt's eschewal of the usual illegal cash portion which Mónica had already explained to me, I wondered what Fede stood to gain from the sale. It would have been rude to ask, but I did mention it during the short drive home. Mónica opined that he was simply doing his aunt a good turn, while Don Andrés suspected that she'd slip him a couple of thousand.

"Oh, who cares?" said Mónica. "Ah, isn't it a great twist of fate that the house seems almost ready-made for guest accommodation, with its own entrance up those steps?"

"Er, not quite ready-made," I said. "More like a blank canvas, in fact, that will cost a lot of money to fill."

She tickled my neck from her cramped rear seat. "There's no hurry."

"I'm glad. Tell me, how on earth did a thousand people use to live in such a small village? Have a lot of houses been pulled down or something?"

"Not at all," said Don Andrés. "When I was a boy the general decline in Extremadura's population had only just begun. It was in the sixties when the mass exodus to the cities occurred, after Franco's government had finally begun to secure a lot of foreign investment, which went hand in hand with the first real tourism boom. Ah, yes, we'd sometimes stop in Casas de Reina on our bikes after playing in the Roman theatre. That restaurant was just a scruffy bar back then, with sawdust on the floor, but I recall it being full of bronzed peasants, slaking their thirst after a hard day in the fields. There were lots of ragged urchins around too, all amazed by our expensive bicycles, and therein lies the answer to your question, Brian. In most of the houses there'd be at least five or six people, sometimes many more, with up to four generations under the same roof."

Mónica yawned, in anticipation of what was to come, she later told me.

"Ah, yes, those were the days. Every single village in the Campiña Sur was a thriving community. Most of the men still laboured for the landowners, but we took good care of them and no-one starved, not around here, anyway. They were humble, Godfearing folk, most of them content with what they had. Then, one fine day, a restless young fellow takes it into his head to go to seek his fortune in the city. He works like a slave, building blocks of flats, for instance, then comes back with a great wad of pesetas in his wallet, inviting his mates to drinks and telling them that the streets of Madrid or Barcelona are paved with gold. So, then what happens?"

"I think Brian gets the picture, Papá."

"Yes, well, the younger folk all follow in his footsteps and in a single decade *half* of the population has upped sticks and gone off to become cogs in the capitalist machine. Does that answer your question, son?"

"Thoroughly, but I thought it was socialism you hated, rather than capitalism."

Mónica tittered. "He liked *his* sort of capitalism, when his forebears lorded it over their tenants. Isn't that so, Papá?"

He sighed. "Ah, yes, I was born at least a century too late, and now look at me. Reduced to a single suit and without even a motor car."

"You've got a wardrobe full of clothes, and it was your choice to sell that nice Volvo."

"I never could get my head around that blasted one-way system."

"He used to drive the wrong way along our street until the council impounded his car."

"So I sold it in protest. That made the buggers sit up and take notice."

Mónica laughed. "I'm sure they were devastated. Papá just doesn't like change, you see, Brian."

"I gathered."

"Hmm, I hope there's still a bus service to the village, because I intend to visit you regularly."

"I believe they stopped it some time ago. Don't worry, Cristina can bring you now and then."

"I said regularly." He slapped what passed for the dashboard. "I know, I'll buy this funny little thing from Juanjo, then I'll be able to drive over to lend you a hand."

"Do you know how to do building work, Andrés?"

"I used to be very good at supervising it in my younger days."

Having seen how it was done many times by then, I came close to crossing myself.

15

There comes a time in most stories when a leap into the not-too-distant future is advisable. Due to the host of tiresome tasks that we had to do in the coming weeks, I shall fly through that time rapidly, before landing back in the family home just a couple of days before Christmas.

Bureaucracy in Spain is almost the stuff of legend by now, so I'll spare you the details, but I managed to sort out my residence paperwork without having to go to Badajoz as I'd first feared. Opening two bank accounts – an individual and a joint one – was a cinch, and the house purchase appeared to be going smoothly and no more slowly than they generally do in Britain. In the end Fede's aunt had insisted on €77,000 for her former home, so it seemed likely that Don Andrés had been spot on about the two grand reward for her attentive nephew, which we didn't begrudge him at all.

Alas, I was unable obey my son regarding the sale of my house, because when I called the agency they informed me that a tenant had just signed up for six months and given notice on his current flat, so I felt morally obliged to honour the agreement. It didn't really matter, because Mónica and I had decided to put fifty thousand each into our House Fund, to cover the cost of the purchase, fees, necessary furniture, DIY materials and so on. Once we were able to enter our new home, I feared that she might begin to push for the construction of the guest quarters sooner rather than later, but on realising how much work we'd have to do on the main house, she conceded that the first paying guests might not arrive until the spring of 2019, almost a year and a half away.

This came as a relief to me, as you'll have gathered that I was none too keen to shell out a lot of money in order to clutter the place up with strangers who might be noisy or intrusive. I also felt sure that an investment of that nature would take many years to reap any net rewards, so I hoped that in the meantime I'd be able to divert her attention away from that irksome endeavour and onto something more amenable to me. In short, although still as willing as ever to accede to Mónica's every desire, I'd prefer them to be desires that didn't involve having unknown folk clomping around overhead during the best months of the year.

On the other hand, I was almost as eager as her to begin to promote the joys of Badajoz province to the world, despite the fact that Alberto was unable to give us an official start date for our job, citing certain contractual issues that sounded like a lot of hot air to me. I'd wanted to visit Zafra and Jerez de los Caballeros anyway, but as neither of those two interesting towns will play a part in my account, I'll merely point out the salient features of each.

As well as two noble churches plus a couple of smaller ones, Zafra has not one but two noteworthy squares – the Plaza Grande and the Plaza Chica – but the real jewel in its crown is the stunning, fifteenth-century Palacio de los Duques de Feria, also known as El Castillo de Zafra, due to its imposing castellated design. It's well worth a visit and one can even sleep within its walls, in the posh Parador hotel which will set you back a bob or two, especially during the busier times of year. Zafra has bucked the trend in Extremadura by increasing in population over the years to its current sixteen thousand or so inhabitants. Don Andrés put this down to a number of factors, including the unusual dynamism of its economy, the influx of folk from the surrounding villages, the substantial immigrant population, and the return of many exiles after retiring from their jobs in the cities.

Jerez de los Caballeros, further to the west and a mere ten miles from the border with Portugal, is located on a small hill with good views of the wooded sierras to the east and west. Its extensive castle – whose construction commenced in the thirteenth century on the foundations of a Moorish fortress that the reconquering Christians had all but destroyed – outshone its big old churches in my eyes, and being free to enter made our tour of the heavily restored complex especially enjoyable. Some hefty chunks of the old town walls still survive, though of the six gateways only two remain intact, the Puerta de Burgos being the more imposing of the two.

As for the town's population – one of my pet subjects, you'll have realised by now – after a sustained growth from sixteen to twenty thousand in the 1950s, almost half of those inhabitants had cleared out by the early seventies, after which it had remained much the same. Don Andrés put this unusual pattern down to an initial belief that Jerez might be a better bet for the peasants than their impoverished villages, followed by a realisation that the real money was in the faraway cities. Nowadays Jerez seems like a pleasant place to live, as does Zafra, and I'd certainly recommend them as good destinations for the more adventurous expats who wish to immerse themselves in the language and culture, because during much of the year you're unlikely to hear a word of English spoken on the streets.

Much closer to home, we soon hiked up to the substantial ruins of the Castillo de Reina, initially a Moorish citadel reinforced in the twelfth century to repel the marauding Christians, but to no avail, because King Fernando III of Castille – known as The Saint due to his prolonged and bloodthirsty Holy War – sent them packing in 1246. Historical architecture buffs may find the place a bit disappointing, as it's in a mostly ruinous state and the information signs are almost illegible, but if, like me, you go mainly to marvel at the views and soak up the atmosphere, it's a wonderfully tranquil location even in summer. For local people its main attraction is a fifteenth-century hermitage whose builders integrated a few Visigothic columns into its single nave, as between the Romans and the Moors those feisty Germanic folk ruled most of Spain for a couple of centuries.

My somewhat blasé approach to travel writing, as evidenced by those quickfire descriptions, was soon detected by Mónica, upon which she gifted me a nifty little Canon camera with which to take better photos than those I'd achieved on my slightly outdated smartphone. So it was that while she made copious notes on our travels – with the intention of finding something original to say about each place, rather than regurgitating the same boring old info – it was my job to take carefully composed photos which would hopefully enhance the incisive articles she intended to write.

As Christmas approached we both began to doubt if our job was really going to happen, so she intended to collar Alberto during the festive season and get to the bottom of his shillyshallying. During our initial outings we'd enjoyed the process of compiling written and visual information about our destinations, so Mónica had half a mind to begin an independent blog and tell her brother to shelve his bright idea for the time being. Due to our relatively modest outlay on the house, we wouldn't be in dire need of extra income anyway, and I believe that Ben's scathing comments about the nepotistic nature of the venture – which he'd repeated to her in a later conversation, with bells on – had struck a resounding chord and put her off the idea. I didn't really mind either way, as my innate avarice would probably have outweighed any moral scruples, but in the end events took such a radical turn that the dubious scheme seemed of little significance.

And last but not least, about ten days after our initial visit to our future home, Fede gave me a set of keys and carte blanche to do whatever work we wished. After he'd removed a few choice items – mainly religious pictures and other paraphernalia – he even paid for a skip into which we soon dumped a ton of stuff, from horrendous lampshades through ugly crockery to unwanted furniture, enabling us to see more clearly exactly what we'd have to do. At this point our so-far harmonious vision began to diverge somewhat and it soon became clear that my make-do-and-mend attitude didn't tally with her longer-term and essentially more sensible approach.

We did agree that the walls just needed a good scrub and a bit of filler, followed by a fresh coat of paint, but it wasn't long before the first bone of contention appeared right beneath our feet. My 'a few dollops of cement and a spot of grouting' ruse to fix the crackling tiles just didn't wash with Mónica, and she was quick to point out that it wouldn't be long before fresh crackling would necessitate more remedial action, and so on until I saw sense and retiled the floors in each and every room.

This revelation was a great blow to my morale, partly because my tiling CV only contained a single bathroom – the floor and a couple of walls – plus a few of the abovementioned remedial actions. With Christmas looming and most of the painting still to be done, we agreed to mull over the Tiling Question as we worked, but of course every crackle underfoot helped me to reach the inevitable conclusion that I'd eventually have to rip the whole lot up and start afresh, unless I bottled it and got someone in, but again, events conspired to turn a dreaded ordeal into an inconsequential issue.

16

I wasn't too devastated when Ben told me he wouldn't be coming over at Christmas after all, citing woman trouble as the main reason, because he promised to fly out for a week in February instead. Due to my growing anxiety about all the new people I was about to meet, I much preferred this, because the last thing I needed was to have my mischievous son thrown into the potentially stressful mix. In February we'd still be hard at work on the house, so he'd be able to lend us a hand and be rewarded with plenty of slap-up meals and a few pleasant excursions, I thought as I ran through the notes I'd made regarding the visitors, some of whom would be staying for a long weekend – with Christmas Day falling on the Monday – while others would remain to see in the new year, overlapping in some cases with those who'd be there for the Day of the Kings on January 6th, after which we'd be able to return to our peaceful, industrious life.

"I don't know why you have to make notes at all," Mónica said as we sat in the parlour with her parents on our last quiet evening for a while.

"I'm not very good at remembering names. I know those of your siblings and their spouses, I think, but the thirteen grandchildren and five great-grandchildren will be too much for me, and I don't want to seem rude."

She smiled. "They won't all be here at once, and some of them will spend a lot of time at Edu's anyway."

Doña Luisa sighed. "Why they have to hide out in that ugly house, I don't know."

"For one thing the bedrooms are warmer there, Mamá," she said, though the truth was that some of them had become a bit fed up of their parents' bickering and preferred to do their own thing most of the time. They liked to catch up with their friends, and it was a curious fact that the grown-up grandchildren who had never lived in Llerena had good friends there who had also been born elsewhere, which seemed to prove Mónica's point about the strong pull of the place.

"Although I'm eager to see my wonderful family, in a way I'll be glad when it's all over," said Don Andrés. "I feel that the house you've bought has given me a sense of purpose for the first time in a while, and I'm looking forward to driving over to help you out whenever I feel fit enough."

"You're in much better shape now, Papá, mainly due to your new diet, so don't spoil it by gorging yourself and drinking like a fish over the holidays."

"Hmm, yes, last year I overindulged and paid for it later." He peered at me over his reading specs. "First the old stomach ulcer began to play up, then my blood pressure rose alarmingly. When my rheumatism had finally eased off in the spring, the doctor told me that my diabetes had got worse, and by the time my new tablets kicked in, my annual bout of gout began."

"A rough year," I said.

"Yes, and now that I've got used to eating fodder for breakfast, plus all the other restrictions that your tiresome woman has imposed on me, I must say that I am loath to undo all the good work by stuffing myself with goodies as I usually do."

"You should follow Mamá's example. In the holidays she indulges in the occasional glass of cava and eats a few more sweets than usual, but nothing excessive."

"Bah, your mother's always been blessed with good health. Hardly seen a doctor in her life." He nudged me, as he often did. "Do you know, Brian, that whenever she suffered from… certain ailments, she'd consult the priest rather than her doctor."

"Shut up, Andrés," she snapped, then smiled at me wearily. "I've always believed that the good Lord watches over us. If one lives in a clean, healthy way, it is His greatest desire to grant us a long life."

"Ha, then where was *He* during our childhood, when the peasants were still dying of cholera, typhoid, diphtheria and even smallpox, eh?"

She sniffed. "Things soon improved."

Now it was Mónica's turn to nudge me. "Yes, especially after our democratic government passed the General Health

Law of 1986. Only then were the workers and peasants* treated in the same way as the wealthy."

(*It's high time I pointed out that the Spanish word for peasant, campesino, isn't used in an especially derogatory way.)

Doña Luisa sniffed again. "The socialists made much of that law, but our health services had become quite good before it." She turned to me. "What *had* changed during the decade since Franco died was that the cities had become flooded with drugs. Even a few young Llerenenses were said to have died after taking that awful heroin. I'm not against democracy, in principle, as the alternative could well be worse, but I do know that during the old days people obeyed the law and none of those horrible substances were to be found in Spain."

Don Andrés laughed as he donned his figurative liberal hat. "No, but millions were still in exile, scared to come home because their parents had been on the wrong side during the war."

"Oh, don't talk rubbish, Andrés. You know perfectly well that–"

"Enough… por favor," I interjected with the modicum of authority that I'd acquired after spending so many evenings with my warm feet under that heavy tablecloth. "In this season of peace and goodwill, let's not argue."

Mónica tittered. "Amen."

Don Andrés leant back and patted his slightly reduced belly. "Ah, bring on next year and all the exiting activity that I'm so looking forward to. Are you going to buy that car then, Brian?"

I told him that the Opel Astra estate which Juanjo had offered us at a good price seemed like the best available option, due to its load-carrying capacity.

"Good, then I'll take that Dyane off his hands and be able to whizz over to see you whenever I want."

"Then return home using the one-way system correctly," said M.

"Of course. I feel that my days of rebelling against authority may be over. Now that I seem less likely to die any time soon, I must look to the future with valour. I intend to make up for the egotism that I've been guilty of in recent years by helping my fellow man, namely you two."

I eyed the ceiling and mumbled a prayer.

Mónica joined me upstairs only a few moments after I'd entered the bedroom, our sleeping apart charade having become a mere formality by then. On seeing my furrowed brow, she instinctively knew that it wasn't the impending visitors who were worrying me.

"Don't fret about Papá. He'll soon tire of driving over to see us every day."

"I do hope so, really, because he won't be much help and you know I like to work quietly away."

She snuggled up to me. "He's found some old overalls in his wardrobe. He says he doesn't know how they got there, but he intends to start wearing them."

"Oh, God."

"I believe it'll be a good thing. He's limited himself to giving advice so far, but if we hand him a paintbrush and tell him to get cracking, he'll soon tire of such an unfamiliar task."

"Physical work?"

"Yes, then he'll leave us alone, at least some of the time."

"Oh, I do like your dad, and I'm really pleased that his health has improved, but... well, you know I came here to make a life with you, not your parents."

"And that's what we'll do."

17

I've decided to describe the Christmas holidays in broad strokes, not wishing to clutter up my narrative with tiresome descriptions of people who were yet to make an impact on my life. The main festivities in Spain take place on Christmas Eve, New Year's Eve and the Day of the Kings. They all involve substantial feasts which are mainly differentiated by the type of sweets consumed, and on New Year's Eve one has to attempt to eat twelve seedless grapes while the clock is striking twelve. On Christmas Day, New Year's Day and on the eve of the Day of the Kings, feasts of somewhat less importance are enjoyed, and nowadays presents are given at Christmas as well as on the more traditional sixth of January, due to the heinous influence of those dratted Americans, Don Andrés opined. Our feasts were prepared by the womenfolk, of course, while us chaps helped out when required, some more than others, though I believe I was among the more willing dogsbodies.

Alejandro was absent once again, preferring to spend Christmas in Germany, but the others all turned up, usually for a few days. Alberto was unable to enlighten us regarding the commencement of our joint job, but rather than telling him that we'd manage without it, Mónica preferred to see what transpired, as if nothing else it would be a lesson to him not to promise things that he couldn't fulfil. His wife Susana was a stolid, unassuming lady and their three adult children, though polite enough, paid little attention to their aunt's English bloke who tended to stay on the periphery of their often deafening conversations in the large sitting room, where a roaring fire consumed a vast amount of wood, Don Andrés grumbled to me at least once a day.

Alberto and Susana's son, also Alberto, had two of the five little grandkids, while three belonged to Mari Carmen and her husband Jorge's two daughters, who spent much of their time at brother Edu's house, along with Edu's long-suffering wife Rosa and their pro-Catalan son Marco, who was studying Spanish law. Felipe from Salamanca and his noisy (rather than dozy) wife Paula spent a lot of time with their friends, while their teenage son Zefe took every opportunity to go out and get drunk with his own pals, often arriving home in the early hours.

Now that I've dispatched the more distant relatives – in both senses of the word – I'll turn my attention to the two sisters who were to play a more significant part in our lives. Cristina attended about half of the feasts and Juanjo just two, along with their taciturn son Santi, a policeman in Cordoba, and their spirited daughter Olivia who was studying to be a nurse in Badajoz. It seemed strange to see Cristina in the role of doting mother rather than dutiful daughter, as since our arrival in Llerena she'd visited the family home most days and eaten so many meals with us that I'd begun to think of her nuclear family as a semi-fictional entity.

The lovely Lourdes came home without her generally loathed, baboon-like husband for the first time and spent a whole fortnight in Llerena, staying with a close friend and her family for several nights. Her bright, attractive daughter

Ana, who was studying business administration in Madrid, soon became my favourite of the grandkids, partly because she had more time for me than the others. One afternoon after a moderately heavy feast she found me skulking in the parlour and proceeded to give me a thorough quizzing about my long career in furniture.

On telling her that I was still replying to old George's secretary's emails on a regular basis – having refused to listen to him on the phone more than once a month – she remarked that since I appeared to have been keen on my work, it seemed strange that I'd never wished to set up my own company.

"Oh, it crossed my mind a few times in the early days, but one gets used to receiving a salary and only having to worry about one aspect of the business, in my case sales," I said in my now fairly fluent Spanish.

The fresh-faced girl smiled. "I'm studying business because I want to have my own, not to work for someone else, though I'll probably do that at first to get some experience."

"Yes, that's probably the best idea. Do you have any business ideas right now?"

"Oh, I was thinking about things like pest control, industrial cleaning or manufacturing fertilizer."

"What?"

She chuckled. "Not seriously, but my idea is to do something unusual that others might not think of or wish to do. The trouble with the obvious business ideas is that too many people want to get involved."

"Hmm, such as rural tourism, I suppose."

"Ha, yes, like you two. I believe rural lodging could work well in that village, though I doubt you'll make much money, not for a long time anyway."

I smiled. "My thoughts entirely, though don't tell your aunt that."

She frowned. "I've been thinking about my mother's situation too. She works as a freelance writer, as you know, but she doesn't get commissions all the time, so she doesn't earn as much as she'd like. I hope that in the future we might be able to work together in some way, so I always bear her in mind when I'm thinking about possible business ventures."

I smiled. "I'll have a think too and let you know if I come up with anything interesting."

"Gracias. You may find that you also need something to do, once you've renovated the house. You are still quite young, after all."

My cheeks flushed youthfully as I told that at present I had rural tourism on the brain, but that I too suspected that other, less obvious lines of work might have more potential. I said this partly to please her, as she and her mother, along with Cristina and Don Andrés, were my favourite family members, but I also had an inkling that once the main house was finished I might find myself at a loose end. The fact that I didn't mind continuing to advise my former boss and colleagues suggested that my will to work remained quite strong, although I'd told old George that I wanted him to pester me less as the coming year progressed, because my ongoing goodwill had its limits.

He'd already suggested that I set up a branch of the company in Spain, but I'd pointed out that Spaniards were quite handy furniture-makers too, before mentioning three middle-aged brothers who had a longstanding carpentry workshop in the village and turned out some really good stuff. Also, with the dreaded Brexit agreement looming, I'd told the old workaholic that we'd soon find ourselves at a disadvantage in the community which we'd so foolishly chosen to abandon, thanks to short-sighted patriots like him.

I didn't like his suggestion anyway, but I found Ana's eagerness quite contagious and decided to make it a new year's resolution to don the old thinking cap and come up with a brilliant business idea that she, her mother, and maybe even Mónica and I could develop. Her quirky ideas – pest control and so on – had reminded me of the old Yorkshire expression, 'Where there's muck, there's brass', and while rural tourism sounded ever so pleasant, I couldn't help but think that a less appealing line of work might be more lucrative, although of course the Iberian pig industry was still out of the question, unless we began to breed them as pets.

I made a quip about this to Ana, and after laughing politely she told me that she had been giving some thought to other types of animals, such as chickens. She believed that many suburbanites in Spain might like the idea of keeping a few, especially those people who still remembered the old ways, and if a company were able to provide them with the whole setup, from the cages to a modest consignment of birds, they might be prepared to shell out quite a bit of cash to become poulterers at the drop of a hat.

"That sounds like a great idea to me," I said sincerely.

"Hmm, it isn't bad. Imagine an attractive website with a video showing a contented family gathered around their chicken coop (gallinero) at the bottom of their garden, with their lovely chalet visible in the background. Presented in such a way and making good use of social media, the idea might catch on, but when I finish my degree in summer I won't have enough money to put it into practice."

Impressed by her vision, I told her I'd give it and similar ideas some thought, then Don Andrés stormed in, wailing about the cost of the fresh load of firewood that he'd had to order, thus breaking up our constructive tête-à-tête. We did have time to exchange email addresses before he whisked her away to play cards, a popular pastime between meals which I didn't partake in, partly because I didn't understand the colourful Spanish playing cards.

So the holidays passed by pleasantly enough, and I'd soon lose the three pounds I'd gained when I returned to my usual healthy diet. Don Andrés, his food and drink consumption policed by the Tiresome Trio (Las Tres Pesadas), as he called Cristina, Lourdes and Mónica, had gained less than a kilo and told me he was dying to get stuck into some real hands-on work for the first time in his life.

"You can be my labourer when I begin to lay tiles in the downstairs bedroom," I said on the evening after the last visitor had finally left, by which time I'd convinced Mónica that a wholesale replacement of the floors wasn't our top priority, but that we'd get them all done eventually.

"And what will my labours consist of?"

I told him.

He puffed out his broad chest. "Yes, I think I can manage some of those things, though I don't think I've knelt down since I was forced to go to church a couple of years ago, but even I can't avoid attending funeral services." He rubbed his soft hands together. "Will you hand over that little French car this week then?"

Yes, I should be getting the Astra tomorrow."

Mónica asked her mother if she'd feel lonely with Papá out of the house all day long.

"I very much doubt that he'll have much staying power, dear. Ah, it's nice to relax after the holidays, though I've enjoyed myself immensely. Everybody seems to be doing all right, though that scamp Zefe needs to slow down, or he may turn into a terrible drunk like his maternal grandfather. I've spoken to Felipe about this and told him that I'll pray for the boy. Lourdes seems far happier without the dreadful Daniel."

(I instantly pictured a baboon, much like Reggie Perrin's visions of his mother-in-law as a hippopotamus.)

"I've invited her to stay here to think over her future, rather than buying an apartment in Cáceres right away. I doubt she'll come, though she knows her room is ready for her, so we can only hope that God gives her guidance. Oh, I feel weary tonight, so I think I'll turn in early. Good night and God bless to you all."

We wished her goodnight and went on talking about the house which we hoped to move into within a few weeks.

18

Although over three years have passed, it still saddens me to write that Doña Luisa died that night. When Don Andrés entered her room early in the morning, her eyes were closed and her face wore a serene expression, but even before touching her he knew that she'd passed away. It later transpired that she'd had a fatal heart attack, though her composed appearance suggested that she may have had time to pray as her life ebbed away, though without her precious rosary beads.

The house was soon in a flurry of activity and I stood by as the emergency services performed their tasks, while Mónica and her father sat alone in the parlour, overcome by grief and the terrible shock of her sudden demise. When it became clear that the coroner and other officials were happy for me to act as a representative of the family, I became infused with a feeling of self-importance as I bustled around with a grim frown on my face, obtaining the necessary signatures from Don Andrés and taking it upon myself to break the news to Cristina and Lourdes.

When Samira arrived and I told her the sad tidings, she burst into tears and lamented the death of such a lovely lady. After composing herself she went to give her condolences to Don Andrés and Mónica, before beginning to prepare the rooms for the flood of arrivals which we expected. Alicia was also distressed by the passing of her demanding boss, and when I made a rueful quip about the tinkling bell she assured me that she'd enjoyed hearing its sound, as she'd loved to spend a few minutes chatting to the señora in the parlour.

She wiped her eyes. "Such a kind, noble lady. It won't be the same here without her. Now, you must give me some money to do a big shop, as all her children will be arriving today."

"All of them? Won't some come later, before the funeral?"

She regarded me as if I were an especially strange kind of Martian. "In your country, I don't know, but in Spain we all gather round when a loved one dies."

"We do too," I lied, as when my own mother had died three years earlier, a lightning trip to the crematorium was all that some relatives had managed.

She perused my unswollen eyes. "Aren't you upset, Brian?"

I sniffed. "Of course I am, but someone must remain calm and organise things."

She scoffed. "Don't worry, I will. Now, please get me some money while I'm offering my condolences to the family."

So I nipped upstairs and emptied my wallet, as it was no time to bother Don Andrés about such trivial matters, and he rarely had more than a few euros anyway. As they were about to take the body away, the priest arrived, having been summoned by one of the officials who had worshipped with Doña Luisa. Unable to give her the last rites, he mumbled a few prayers before going to commiserate the family. Cristina had arrived by then and the stout clergyman's soothing words seemed to console them a little. When they began to pray around the table, I seated myself on the edge of an armchair and adopted a suitably pious posture, peering up to see Don Andrés praying as fervently as the girls, before crossing himself and kissing his fingers with apparent devotion, a far cry from his usual yawns, nose-picking and occasional farts.

Lourdes was the next to arrive, followed by Alberto and Felipe. I accompanied each of them to the parlour, saying the usual trite things, then left them to it, as it was becoming clear that the presence of us in-laws wasn't yet required. After finally managing to get a decent fire going in the large sitting room, I opened the door to Mari Carmen and a slim, handsome fellow who turned out to be Alejandro.

I gawped at him as I shook his hand. "But... but how did you get here from Germany so quickly?"

"I was in Barcelona for work, so I drove to Madrid, picked up my sister, and here we are." He shook his head and began to weep. "Oh, how I regret not coming at Christmas now."

As Mari Carmen led him away I imagined that he also felt guilty about not having planned to fit in a visit to Extremadura during his work trip, but it turned out that he'd intended to surprise them that weekend, so he was doubly devastated by his mother's death.

When a distraught Edu arrived at about three, I persuaded the huddled mourners to go through to the large sitting room to have a bite to eat. Alicia, Samira and I had formed an efficient team by then, and after Samira had collected her two kids from school, the three of them repaired to the servants' quarters to make the beds, because husbands, wives and grandkids were expected to arrive the next day and hardly anyone would be staying at Edu's house. When I pointed out to my co-workers that their scheduled hours were over, they told me they didn't care about that, because Doña Luisa would have wished them to rally round.

Notwithstanding the autopsy which was to be carried out, Alicia assured me that the body would soon be taken to the tanatorio, or funeral parlour, and by Friday at the latest the burial would take place. I was glad about this, because when the two kind ladies finally departed, I soon found myself in a state of limbo, as I didn't wish to intrude on the family too much, but nor did it feel right to skulk around on my own. When they spread themselves out in the two rooms I was more inclined to mingle, but I still felt like the odd man out and, for lack of anything better to say, kept asking people if they wanted anything. My point of view here may seem egotistical, but it's the only one I have and it was certainly strange to find myself in a situation that I could scarcely have imagined happening to me a few months earlier.

I felt saddened by Doña Luisa's sudden death, of course, but we'd never grown close and my main concern was to comfort those who were dear to me, though even my beloved remained distant throughout that tragic day. Young Ana arrived in the evening and after greeting everyone and shedding a few tears, she suggested that the two of us go out for a while.

"Can we do that?"

"Of course we can. Grandfather just told me how wonderfully supportive you've been. He thinks it's about time you had a break from all this, so get your jacket and we'll be off."

"Muy bien."

After a bracing walk around the chilly square, we entered a bar behind the church where the friendly owner Jacinto always made me feel welcome. I expected him to crack a joke about me turning up with an even younger beauty than usual, but he greeted me gravely and told me he'd been sad to hear about the death of Mónica's mother.

"Oh, gracias. Did you know her?"

"Everybody here knew Doña Luisa. She used to come to drink an infusion after church sometimes. Such a fine lady." He smiled at my companion. "I'm sorry for your loss, Ana."

"Gracias, Jacinto."

"The drinks are on me tonight."

Realising what a tight-knit community Llerena was, once we'd sat down with our beers I asked Ana if she expected a lot of people to attend the funeral.

"I expect many will call in at the wake to pay their respects, though only those closer to her will go to the church service, while the burial will be for family and intimate friends."

On enquiring about the wake, she explained that on the afternoon and evening before a funeral, family members watched over the deceased in the funeral parlour, though nowadays people weren't expected to stay overnight as they did in the old days, when the coffin had usually remained at home.

"Surely you have wakes in England too, Brian."

"I've never attended a proper one, though Catholics might still have them." I sighed. "I wonder what will happen now."

She smiled. "In what respect?"

"Oh, everything, really. I wonder how Don... your grandfather and the others will take it."

She chuckled grimly. "I remember grandfather once talking about all the things he'd get up to if his bossy wife weren't around, but of course he was certain that he'd die first, having so many incurable ailments. Last spring he really was quite ill and many of us came to see him, fearing the worst. I remember him saying several times as he lay suffering that we must take care of Luisa after he'd gone."

"And what was wrong with him that time?"

"A suspected heart attack which a young doctor wasn't confident enough to rule out, but it turned out to be a terrible case of indigestion that sent pains all over his chest. I think he truly believed he was dying, and all he could think of was his wife. How ironic it seems to tell this tale now." She dabbed her eyes with a tissue. "I'll say one thing though. It's great that you and Mónica are living here. Without you... well, I guess Mónica would have come straight home, as she didn't like it much in Manchester, but it's better this way, as the two of you will be able to keep him occupied."

I told her that this had been in the offing anyway, but I doubted that he'd feel like partaking in a house renovation for a long time.

"The sooner the better, really. I suppose it's premature to speak about this now, and I'm hardly experienced in these matters, but life goes on and I feel that it'll be crucial for him to keep busy." She looked around the quiet, well-lit bar. "Or he may spend his time here and elsewhere, then we'll soon have another funeral to attend."

I recalled Don Andrés's kind words and thoughtfulness regarding my hectic day. "We'll make it our priority to keep him occupied, at our house or wherever else he wishes to be."

Just then Cristina walked in, ordered a whisky and water, and joined us at the corner table. She'd applied a little makeup to brighten up her sallow cheeks and seemed determined to put on a brave face in public. She had some news too, as Lourdes had decided to come to stay in Llerena for an indefinite period. Ana seemed pleased about this, as her mother and father had been finding cohabitation difficult since they'd chosen to go their separate ways. I still struggled to link the supposedly baboon-like man with his lovely daughter and had to warn myself more than once not to put my foot in it by making some unfortunate wisecrack.

Then Lourdes herself walked in, having applied a little makeup, and ordered a gin and tonic.

"We can't all stay in that house for three or four days," she explained.

I smiled. "I believe you are coming to live here."

She shrugged. "More or less. Given the situation, it seems like a logical thing to do."

"We're all grateful," said Cristina. "Papá is going to be demanding now, bless him, but between us we'll try our best to cheer him up and keep him busy."

Then Mónica walked in, having applied a little makeup, and ordered a vodka and orange, a strange choice for a non-drinker and one which took me back to my younger days, when it had been a popular tipple among the young damsels of Kendal.

She squeezed my neck as she sat down. "You've been marvellous today, Brian."

"I've mainly been obeying Alicia's orders, and Samira's too."

"They've been so kind," she said, wiping away a tear.

Cristina chuckled. "Alicia didn't like Samira at first, as she's not fond of Moroccans, but they were soon getting along fine under the watchful eyes of Mamá, as Papá often threatened to ravish them both."

There followed one of those strange mirthful spells which sometimes punctuate the initial mourning period, as Doña Luisa's daughters swapped tales about their parents' antics over the years, like the time when Don Andrés had brought home an old pal from his military service days and proceeded to infuriate his wife by reminiscing about all the wenches they'd bedded, while the poor man swore that it was all a pack of lies.

All too soon it was time to return home, where the others had been at the whisky, but I doubt any of them slept much more soundly for it, judging by their haggard faces the next morning. I too had a restless night alone in my room, tossing, turning, and selfishly wondering how Doña Luisa's death was going to affect our plans.

19

The following day most of the spouses arrived, and on the eve of the funeral Alejandro's wife Irma and their son Kaspar finally made it after a tiring journey from Monchengladbach. The pale boy of eleven looked uncomfortable among so many noisy Spaniards whose tactility seemed to annoy him, so perhaps in Germany the kids aren't kissed, hugged, prodded and pinched nearly so much. All the older grandchildren came too, some with their partners, though four of the five great-grandkids had been left with relatives. During this time the whole house seemed like a human beehive, and although the women took over most of the cooking, there was still plenty for Alicia, Samira and me to do. Due to my willing servitude, I believe the family began to look upon me as some sort of saintly figure, but the truth was that I preferred to bustle around than sit about with the others, going over the same ground time and time again.

I believed that Don Andrés was finding it all a terrible strain, as they didn't leave him alone for a single moment. At the wake, after the last passing visitors had left, he confirmed this to me as we sat in a corner of the multi-denominational chapel, sipping whiskies from the adjacent bar. By then I was getting used to the feel of my borrowed suit, but the sight of Doña Luisa's face in the open coffin, surrounded by flowers in a large glass display cabinet, didn't cease to disturb me a little. I mentioned this.

"Ah, yes, it's the Catholic way of making a loved one's death even more unbearable. Although a fine tribute in some ways – and I must say they've made her up beautifully – I'll be glad when she's finally taken out of the limelight that she never sought in life. Tomorrow you'll see our preferred burial method which other foreigners I've known found quite unsettling, though it saves space and is less fuss in the long run."

"Do you mean the burial niches?"

"Indeed I do. The coffin is pushed inside and the gravestone cemented over the opening." He sighed. "It's not exactly earth to earth, is it? But my wife wished it this way, so her desire must be respected." He squeezed my hand. "As for me, I wish to go up in flames like a Viking warrior. Then you can place the urn with my ashes in a place of prominence and always remember what a wonderful man I was."

"We will, but not for a long time."

The previous day when someone had made a similar comment, he'd begun to weep and said that he wasn't long for this world, but now he leaned closer and told me that he was keener than ever to help us with the house reforms.

"I'm glad."

"Not just yet, you understand, because I may not feel up to it for a while, and one must abide by the social norms to some extent, but as soon as I'm able I'll be jumping in that little Citroen and driving over." He leant closer still. "In the end I shan't be buying that car though. I've asked Juanjo to look for a model that I've always desired but have never been allowed to have. I trust that no-one will begrudge an old man his little whim, though Luisa would turn in her grave if death weren't so final and all this talk of an afterlife a lot of mumbo jumbo."

I refrained from mentioning his fervent prayers and instead asked him what sort of car he wished to buy.

"Ah, that's a little secret between Juanjo and me, though he thoroughly approves of my choice and will do his best to find me the best one available." After downing his whisky, he rubbed his hands together. "Life goes on, after all. Get me another drink, son, but hurry back or they'll besiege me again."

On my return with two watery whiskies, he assured me that he meant to go on with his new diet and keep up the walking that he'd begun to do, normally about twenty minutes around the square, but far better than nothing. By this time we were getting a few wry glances from the others, most of whom were looking fidgety and ready to leave, so I asked him if he wished to call it a night.

"When we've drunk these." He took a slurp and wiped his mouth with the back of his hand. "I'm a little tipsy now and my current bravado won't last, but I'm relying on you to buck me up and force me to get up off my arse and do things. I'm pleased that Lourdes is coming home, of course, as it'll be good for her too, but now I'll have two women fussing around me like mother hens, as well as Cristina, Alicia and Samira. Although I'll willingly abide by their dietary regulations, I won't wish to be cosseted like some weary old man." He pointed at the coffin. "Here we are, looking death in the face. Does that scare you, Brian?"

"Well, to be honest I haven't given all that much thought to my own mortality yet."

"At seventy-six one can't avoid it, especially with all my ailments, but I swear that however long the Lord… or whatever allows me to live, I mean to make the most of it."

Feeling a bit tipsy myself, I grasped the end of my thumb and began to work my way through the rest of my fingers. "Gout, probably avoidable. Indigestion, definitely avoidable. Stomach ulcer, denied by the doctors. Your type of diabetes, controllable. Heart murmur, probably a figment of your imagination. High blood pressure, already getting lower. Rheumatism, may improve with exercise."

He laughed. "You've forgotten my varicose veins."

"Operable, though they aren't all that bad." I patted his arm. "I believe you have many active years ahead of you, Andrés."

"God willing." He drained his glass and smacked his lips. "Right, let's get this lot home."

I counted over a hundred people at the funeral service in the magnificent church. The priest had happily acceded to the family's request to hold it there rather than at the tanatorio, because – in Don Andrés's words – Luisa had been one of his best customers, swelling the dwindling ranks of communicants and donating liberally over the years. Needless to say, the bright green Citroen was barred from the funeral cortege, so I climbed into Alberto's BMW and broke the news to him that Mónica was no longer so keen on the job that he'd offered us.

I believe he suppressed a smile of relief, before reminding me that the job was to be for me.

"I know, but it's really a joint venture and she's taken her mother's death badly. She thinks it'll be a long time before she'll feel like visiting different places, so it'll be best if we shelve the project for now."

"What a shame, but why hasn't she mentioned this to me?"

As I'd taken it upon myself to relieve him of the burden of keeping a promise that he was obviously struggling to deliver, I just said that she had other things on her mind. My son's harsh word regarding this blatant favouritism were still bugging me, and I preferred to risk a dressing down by Mónica than suddenly have Alberto come up with the goods and oblige us to go out and earn a salary that we didn't really need. I still intended to encourage her to write a travel blog if she wished, and I'd gladly accompany her all over Extremadura with my new camera, but I wanted this threat of an actual job to be quashed right away.

My initial conversation with Ana had inspired me, you see, and I now felt that a real entrepreneurial endeavour would be more up my street. I'd thought her proposal to provide folk with a comprehensive chicken-coop package a great example of thinking outside the proverbial box, so since then, during my occasional periods of downtime, I'd been racking my brains to come up with a similarly original idea, if only to show her that I too was Dragons' Den material, rather than a guy who'd never had the balls to step out of old George's protective shadow and go it alone.

At the tidy little cemetery just outside town the priest uttered a final prayer as the coffin was slid into the niche, and I eyed the ground as two workmen swiftly cemented a slab over which the gravestone would later be placed. While the family shed yet more tears, I resolved to tell Mónica that I wished to be cremated – many years hence, touch wood – and have her scatter my ashes at our favourite place, wheresoever that may be.

20

In the course of the following day everyone except Lourdes, Ana and Cristina went home, so for the rest of the weekend Don Andrés was accompanied by four women who allowed him little time for solitary contemplation. On Sunday evening he collared me in the passage and told me to grab the car keys, because we were getting the hell out of there for a while.

On the way to Villagarcía de la Torre, a village about five miles along the Zafra road, he drove the Dyane slowly, having scarcely been behind the wheel of a car since he'd sold his Volvo two years earlier, partly because he believed that his recent decline in health was likely to be terminal. When he opined that Juanjo was a very capable mechanic, I said that he'd certainly done a good job on the Dyane, having turned a dilapidated heap into a fine little runner.

"Shame about the paintwork though."

Don Andrés smiled. "Oh, he only touched up the existing mess. He intended to sell it quickly, but he's grown attached to it. Like me, he's fond of old cars, but Cristina won't let him indulge his whim until Olivia has finished her nursing studies." He turned off the deserted main road. "Let's hope no-one knows me in the bar and we can natter about cars like two regular guys."

Glad that we'd found an amenable topic to discuss, over our beers I told him about the rather boring company cars I'd used for the last twenty-odd years, preceded by a rusty Ford Escort and, before my time in Valencia, an even rustier Mini.

"Ah, cars had far more character in those days, and of course rust wasn't such a problem in most of Spain. I had my trusty Volvo for eight years, and before that an Audi 100 which I'd treated myself to after our household costs had finally diminished. While our children were growing up I had a huge Citroen DS estate with hydropneumatic suspension, and after that a Renault 21 estate." He sipped his beer. "Now *that* Citroen really did have character. Hmm, so tell me about the Tesla."

"Very smooth and quiet, but a bit too futuristic for my liking," I fibbed, as I'd loved driving it, especially at first when there'd been far fewer of them on the roads. "Go on telling me about your cars, Andrés."

"Ah, well, I'm afraid to go back any further, in case I uncover the cake." (Meaning 'spill the beans' in Spanish.)

"What cake… or figurative cake?"

He grinned. "The model I've asked Juanjo to find me is the first car I ever drove. It was my father's, as was the next, and the first one I owned followed the same pattern, as did the second."

"So?"

"So if I reveal any of those cars, knowing me I'll get carried away and uncover the cake. I'm loath to do that, as at times like these one needs things to look forward to, however trivial." He frowned. "In fact I hope Juanjo doesn't find one too soon, as I wish to be in better spirits when it arrives. It would also be unbecoming of me to go driving around with a smile from ear to ear, which I'll undoubtedly do once I'm behind the wheel of that machine. It was when I was driving the first one that Luisa and I began our courtship, you see, so it's going to bring back a lot of fond memories."

"Mightn't it make you sad too?"

He shrugged. "Of course, but what of it? Her life is over, and with her death the main chapter of mine has also closed. I'm already becoming nostalgic, and what better way to celebrate our life together than by... not reliving it, but conjuring up some of our happiest moments, before the blasted kids began to appear, one after the other."

I laughed. "I'm intrigued now. Can't you give me a clue about those early cars?"

He tutted. "No, because through a little investigation you'd soon put two and two together and discover that first one. It's an uncomplicated timeline, you see, because... no, I shan't say another word."

I sipped my beer, gazed through the window at the lamplit cars outside, then began to smile.

"Has an idea occurred to you, Brian?"

"Perhaps." After reminding him of the business schemes which Mónica, me, and later Ana had been coming up with, I asked him if he thought there might be money to made by sourcing and restoring classic cars.

"I expect so, though one sees so few of them these days. Juanjo's the man to ask about that. His tastes are... different from mine. He wishes to purchase one of those old BMWs from the seventies, the 1602 model or similar, he told me, but they're no longer to be found cheaply."

I smiled. "And the car you wish to buy? Are they cheaper?"

He sighed. "The price of 1950s Ferraris is astronomical."

"Eh?"

He grinned. "But the car I wish to buy can be had for between… a reasonably low price and a surprisingly high one, though Juanjo says the latter are in pristine condition and normally kept in collections. I shall be buying mine to drive it, so it needn't be perfect, but it must be as reliable as one can make a car from that era." He rubbed his hands together and sniggered. "The mere thought of it delights me, and God knows, I'll need whatever distractions I can get. Tell me, do you understand the workings of the motor car?"

"Oh, I used to tinker with them a bit, but I haven't for some time, as my company cars rarely broke down and they've become so complicated in recent years. I certainly wouldn't be able to restore one."

"Maybe not, but Juanjo loves to work on old cars. Besides, you and I are experienced in sales, so our… your role in such an initiative would be to sell the restored product."

I smiled. "Would you like to get involved too, Andrés?"

He shrugged. "Oh, I don't know. One must mull over these ideas for a while." With what still seemed to me like a rude gesture, he indicated to the waiter that we'd like two more beers. "The truth of the matter is that you and I lack the necessary knowhow, a potentially disastrous drawback. Juanjo would be a key player in an enterprise of this kind, and although he's eager to get under the bonnet of my car, I doubt he'll wish to clutter up his garage with a lot of old vehicles. Servicing modern cars is his bread and butter, after all, so who knows what he'll think of the idea. Juanjo's not the most forthcoming of men, as you know, and he frequents our house as seldom as possible." He shrugged. "You can ask him what he thinks, but I suggest you allow this enticing plan to mature for a while."

"Yes, I'll do that. Besides, we've got lots of work to do on the house, and Mónica's still keen to do her travel articles, or she will be once she begins to get over the loss of her mother."

"Yes, we're all sad now, but tell her that keeping busy denotes no lack of respect for the deceased. Thank God most people have now dispensed with the loathsome tradition of wearing mourning clothes." He tapped his forehead. "But up here us Spaniards still feel that we have to go about with long faces for months on end. I know Luisa wouldn't want that, and if she is up there looking down on us, her greatest wish will be for the family to get on with their lives and achieve things that she'll be proud of."

I smiled. "Like restoring old cars?"

"Why not? As you know, she preferred the olden days, so to keep those cars on the road will help to conserve those repressive times in the minds of those who do wish to remember them. As for me, I just love the cars."

I ignored the contradictory nature of his statement and we began to speak of other business schemes, including Ana's singular chicken racket. Don Andrés found this amusing and joked that folk might be better off renting a few birds and a cage, because once they found out how noisy and smelly they could be, they'd regret having purchased the whole caboodle. I believe that it was this chicken-related chatter that planted the seed of an idea in my mind which wouldn't actually sprout for another few of weeks, when I had something akin to a eureka moment.

Back at the house, the girls had just rustled up some supper, so we took out seats at the long table, having agreed not to natter on about old cars, as it might seem unseemly and we suspected they wouldn't be interested in that sort of thing anyway. It turned out to be yet another morose gathering and I believe we were all fed up of these collective meals during which we spoke about Doña Luisa or made desultory small talk. Ana tried to get Mónica to tell us about her proposed travel blog, but my sweetheart's heart wasn't in it, so I filled the breach by droning on about the work I planned to do at the house.

Later Mónica came to my room for the first time in a week and I set about trying to cheer her up, but she was so sad that I soon desisted. When I made the mistake of saying that she'd taken her mother's death very hard, she accused me of being a cold-hearted Englishman, before asking me how I'd felt when my own parents had died. She knew that my father's illness had been so long and painful that his passing had been a truly merciful release, while my mother's decline had been more rapid, but she hadn't suffered nearly as much. I now told her that in each case, after the initial blow, I'd tried to immerse myself in my work and that my mourning had been a very up and down affair, with periods of sadness interspersed with happy memories and, as time went on, a gradual acceptance of the fact that they'd gone.

"They married late, so they were both in their eighties when they died," I said after we'd climbed into bed.

"Mamá was only seventy-five."

"Yes, I know."

"That's not so old these days."

I rehearsed a reply in my mind and decided to risk it. "That's true, but it should be some consolation to know that she's been spared the trials of real old age. She had a good life and... well, it's those who are left behind who really suffer."

She gazed at the ceiling. Believing that my consoling words had gone down well, I tried to come up with another philosophical gem.

"Brian?" she said to the lampshade.

"Yes, love?"

"You're an idiot."

I sighed. "Yes, I suppose I am."

"But I love you."

"And I love you too, more than ever."

"Ah, just give me a little time and I'll be my old self again."

"I'm sure you will."

She wept softly on my shoulder for a while, then fell asleep in my arms.

21

On Monday morning as I walked to Juanjo's garage on the north-western edge of town, I breathed in great gulps of cold air and greeted many of the people I passed. It was a relief to leave that big old house and get back to work on ours, but first I had to collect the red Astra estate which Juanjo had acquired on a recent trip to Cáceres, where an old schoolmate of his worked at the Opel dealership. Four years old and with only 27,000 kilometres on the clock, I was pleased with the spacious, shiny vehicle, but Juanjo remarked that I didn't seem overly excited at the prospect of driving it away.

"Oh, it looks like new and it's just what we need, but these modern cars don't thrill me like the old ones," I said, having prepared that little conversation-starter earlier.

As I'd hoped, he then asked me about the cars I'd owned in my younger days, so I was able to enthuse about my rusty Escort and rustier Mini, mentioning a few repairs that I'd managed to carry out myself.

When his usually impassive eyes became wistful, I told him I'd been talking to Don Andrés about the car he was awaiting.

"Did he tell you what it is?"

"No, he wants it to be a surprise, but he did say that you were keen to get your hands on a 1602 or a 2002," I said, omitting the name of the manufacturer in order to imply that I was a fellow classic car buff.

His brown eyes lit up as he lit a fag on the cramped forecourt of the modern, purpose-built unit. "I hope to be allowed to get one next year, when I turn fifty. I may end up buying it in Germany, as there aren't so many in Spain and they ask a fortune for the best ones." He took a long drag and smiled as he exhaled. "I'll locate a few online, hopefully in the same city, then ask Alejandro to accompany me to see them."

"Will you buy one in really excellent condition?"

He shook his head. "No, far too dear. As long as the bodywork's sound and the engine's in decent shape, I'll be able to restore it myself." He shrugged. "I guess that's part of the fun. I'll leave the pristine classics for those with deep pockets and little mechanical knowhow."

"Once we've finished the house – or the main house, as Mónica calls it – I may think about buying an old car too."

"What kind?"

"I don't know yet," I said truthfully, as I was aiming to power-steer the conversation around to the project that Don Andrés and I had discussed.

"In that case, I'm not sure you ought to bother. To buy a classic car just for the sake of it can be an expensive mistake, in my experience. I believe it's the nostalgic desire to reacquaint oneself with a vehicle that was once significant that makes it worthwhile."

"To have owned it before, you mean?"

"Not necessarily. I've never owned a 1602, but when I was doing my apprenticeship in Zafra, a customer at the garage had a beautiful blue one. He was a local pijo (a snobbish, reactionary type) and I hated his guts, but I loved that car and thought I deserved one more than he did, as the fool didn't even know how to check the oil." He shrugged. "My first car was a clapped-out Renault Four which I restored quite well, so I'm fond of those too, but it's the BMW that I really wish to own. Right, I'd better get back to work, Brian."

So I left it at that, because I'd realised that the time wasn't yet ripe to broach the subject of classic car commerce in more general terms. I believed he might have disparaged the idle dreaming of two wannabe dealers and also baulked at the idea of shouldering the burden of the restorations. No, our best bet would be draw him into our scheme gradually, so as I drove away in my boring modern car, I pondered on the possible classics I could become enthusiastic about as soon as Don Andrés's old SEAT 600 arrived.

I'd put two and two together by then, you see, and realised that he must have been referring to the first and only

Spanish car brand, apart from Pegaso, who made mainly trucks. SEAT was set up in the 1950s in partnership with Fiat, and as Don Andrés had been born in 1941, it seemed likely that his father would have snapped up the first truly affordable Spanish car after its release in 1957. His old man must have been quite wealthy and could probably have afforded a foreign car, but the fact that Don Andrés had mentioned a pattern when referring to the first four cars he'd driven made me assume that his father had been a patriot who had supported the Spanish company. I couldn't be sure, of course, but all the signs suggested that my old pal would soon be whizzing around town in one of those dinky things which certainly put a smile on one's face.

After a trip to the building supplies yard and another to the hardware store, I drove to Casas de Reina and went on painting the kitchen whose solid but antiquated units were to remain for the time being. We'd already ditched the rusty gas cooker and would soon order an electric one, as gas was only available in bottles, so the less we used the better, I believed. To this end we planned to purchase a cast iron wood-burning stove for the hearth, as neither of us felt like investing in central heating until we'd lived there for a while.

Mónica only came to the house once that week, to show it to Lourdes, who thought it had potential both as a home and a source of supplementary income. When I mentioned that it might take several years to recoup the costs of the building work, she disagreed, before declaring that if we could rent the apartment out most weeks from Easter to October, we might make as much as fifteen or even twenty thousand in the first year alone.

After dropping my scraper, I politely asked her how she'd reached that mouth-watering figure.

"Easy. €800 multiplied by twenty weeks makes €16,000."

Mónica's ominous glance made me desist from asking her who the hell was going to traipse all the way to a nondescript village in Extremadura to shell out so much money on a modest apartment with no view to speak of, except perhaps in the holiday month of August. Instead I tried my best to sound enthusiastic about her optimistic vision, mainly to cheer up my black-clad girlfriend.

"He's got no faith in the project," Mónica muttered. "And I believe he has his mind on other schemes."

I pointed my scraper at the ceiling, above which they expected to hear the patter of miscellaneous feet during half of the year. "We can get the builders in whenever you wish. It oughtn't to cost more than a season's rent, so we might as well get cracking right away," I said, striving to erase all signs of irony from my eyes.

By way of reply, Mónica began to hustle her sister out of the scruffy shell of a bedroom.

"I'll pay for it myself, to prove that I'm willing," I cried to the receding figures. On hearing my name being taken in vain in the hallway, I hurried out and offered to buy them a drink in the bar.

"The *bar*?" Mónica asked rhetorically, as if I'd suggested a threesome in a nearby brothel.

I refrained from mentioning the drinks they'd knocked back in the local bar on that first evening. "Just for a coffee," I pleaded.

Lourdes flicked a speck of dust from her black jacket. "I suppose we could."

My indignant gal stomped out, her sister shrugged, and I went on scraping at the old paint with a vengeance, feeling that I'd been treated with undue harshness.

Mónica doesn't mind me having a laugh at her expense here, because she realises that she was in a weird frame of mind during the two or three weeks following her mother's death. She later put it down to a subconscious guilt complex caused by her having spent two years abroad without achieving anything of note, when she could have been in Llerena, keeping her mother company while she planned her next move. When I pointed out – at the time of writing – that had she done that she wouldn't have met me, she opined that fate can work in mysterious ways and we might well have met somewhere else, but I digress.

So I plodded on mostly alone for another fortnight. Don Andrés drove over occasionally in the Dyane to see how I was getting on, but he was having a rough time too, feeling terribly down most days, though that didn't stop him from quaffing the odd beer in the bar. At home of an evening, Lourdes was slightly more successful than me at lifting them from their melancholy state. She too was feeling the loss of her mother, of course, but she was quite busy with her writing and seemed to be showing those two that the light at the end of the tunnel wouldn't be too long in coming. Ana made the long trip from Madrid one weekend and her agreeable presence was appreciated by us all. Cristina was also bearing up well, with her administrative work at the town hall helping to pass the time, so I believe that it gradually dawned on Don Andrés and Mónica that their idleness was only exacerbating their morose state of mind.

Towards the end of January, Mónica began to don her scruffy clothes and lend me a hand at the house that would soon be officially ours. Then, one cold, sunny Tuesday in early February a new arrival in the family began to have a remarkably favourable effect on us all.

22

I'd just laid the last tile in the downstairs bedroom and was admiring my first completed floor when I heard the insistent sound of beeping. That's no modern car horn, I thought as I quickly washed my hands, before making haste to get my first glimpse of Don Andrés's SEAT 600.

At first I thought the shiny black four-door saloon was an old Ford Popular, but the badge on the bonnet told me that my conjecture hadn't been entirely wrong.

"It's a SEAT 1400," Juanjo said as I admired the chrome bumper and radiator grill.

"A 1400A, to be exact," said a beaming Don Andrés, whose trimmed moustache, tweed suit and flapping overcoat complemented the vintage car beautifully. "Made in 1955, two years after the first model came out to great acclaim, especially from the government. Few Spaniards could afford one in those days, but many thousands were used by the police, civil servants, doctors, and the like. They even made an elongated version to be used as an ambulance." He stroked the single wing mirror attached to the driver's door. "It's based on a Fiat design, of course, but in the huge Barcelona factory they manufactured every component bar the light bulbs, quite an achievement in a still far from industrialised country. My father owned a Citroen B11 before this one, a superior car in many ways, but after he bought his first SEAT he never looked back."

I confessed to having expected to see a SEAT 600.

He chuckled. "He offered to buy my mother one of those, but she preferred to be driven around. Ah, I remember our first trips in our 1400, also a black one. In Llerena cars were already quite a common sight, but in the villages the kids would run after us along the dusty streets, and the peasants felt proud that at last us Spaniards could make our own cars." He patted the solid roof. "Right, come on, let's go for a spin."

I slapped my dusty jeans. "I'm a bit dirty."

"Don't worry, the seats are covered with good old-fashioned vinyl, though they aren't original."

After brushing myself down and locking the front door, I settled into the squishy rear seat and Don Andrés fired up the throaty engine. On the way to the bar in Villagarcía de la Torre he confessed to having paid €9,000 for the car which he and Juanjo had gone to buy in Seville, before having it trailered to the garage, just in case. After a thorough inspection and service, Juanjo had deemed it perfectly roadworthy, and the few blemishes on the bodywork didn't bother its new owner in the least.

He patted the large, slim steering wheel. "But Juanjo has insisted that when I get my 1500, it has to be a better bargain."

"Your what?"

He sniggered. "I have a plan which Juanjo here secretly approves of, though he can't bring himself to admit it."

Juanjo turned to face me. "Our father-in-law's got this crazy idea, Brian, but just now it's impossible to reason with him."

"Oh, there's plenty of method in my madness, as I'll explain to you over a nice cool beer." He shifted from side to side, making the heavy car rock like a boat. "Ah, it's so liberating not to have to wear those stupid seatbelts, isn't it?"

I noticed their absence for the first time. "If one drives carefully, yes."

After leaving the main road, he told us to brace ourselves, as he was about to do an emergency stop. In the event we needn't have bothered, because the car rolled to a halt about thirty yards later.

"Oh, yes, they knew how to make drum brakes back then. None of that ABS nonsense. The engine delivers fifty horsepower and can do over 120 kilometres per hour. I don't think the fuel consumption is too great, but I doubt I'll be making many long trips." He parked outside the bar between two soulless modern cars. "Ha, look, they're already admiring Don Benito."

"What?" I said.

"Who?" said Juanjo.

He moved the curious gearstick on the steering column into neutral, before applying the handbrake. "I've decided to name the car after my father."

"I'd drop the Don, if I were you," said JJ.

"Hmm, yes, I might do that. Benito, yes, that sounds better."

In the bar, after Don Andrés had happily responded to sundry comments about the car, we settled down at a table to drink our beers. There he explained the marvellous idea that he'd had while viewing the other classic cars in the Seville showroom. Among an impressive selection of old vehicles, SEAT was scarcely represented – just a lone 600 besides the 1400 – and it had occurred to him to gradually build up a collection of all the SEAT models from the first one up to the mid-seventies, after which they'd become too modern for his liking.

"I think I'll skip the 600 for now and look for a good 1500, a bigger saloon that my father bought after the 1400. He kept that for many years, but in the meantime SEAT released the 800, a four-door version of the 600, and then the iconic 850, which came as a saloon, a coupé, and the superb soft-top Spyder."

"So which of those cars did you drive?"

"The 1400, the 1500, my own 800, and then an 850 Coupé. After that I was forced to become more practical and bought a second-hand Tiburón (Shark), as the Citroen DS was affectionately known, due to its rather menacing appearance, ha ha."

He was in such an exuberant mood that neither Juanjo nor I wished to bring him down to earth by questioning the wisdom of buying a lot of old cars when he didn't even have a garage in which to store the one he owned. We spoke about Benito – a name he soon abandoned – for a while, then over our second beers he outlined the plan to which he'd evidently been giving a lot of thought. First he made it clear to Juanjo that he didn't expect any more favours from him. He would try to find a cheaper 1500, but his son-in-law would be paid in full for the mechanical overhaul, while a pal of Juanjo's who did car body repairs in Zafra could take care of any cosmetic imperfections.

"I reckon that one of the cars will be safe enough parked outside your house, Brian, and you and Mónica will be welcome to use whichever one I'm not driving at the time. Before I acquire the third one, however, I'll look into buying a safe storage space in Llerena, then I'll be free to expand the collection. How does that sound?"

After raising my drooping jaw, I pointed out that the expense could be considerable.

"Oh, that depends. I'll see how I feel after each purchase. Right now I want to look for a 1500 while I enjoy driving the 1400. It may prove to be a passing whim, a reaction to recent events, but I have the money and I mean to enjoy it. It'll keep me entertained and my expert mechanic assures me that as long as I buy well, the cars are likely to increase in value, isn't that so, Juanjo?"

"Well, classic car prices are rising now, but there'll always be risk involved."

"Ha, risk, he says. Until recently I expected to stretch the leg (kick the bucket) at any moment, and after what happened to my dear Luisa, who's to say that I won't, despite my infernal diet? Besides, the cars will be fully insured for an amount superior to what I pay – a friend of mine will see to that – so I see very little risk at all."

"Neither do I," I said, thinking it a sound plan and a great hobby to keep him busy. It was while he was chewing a mouthful of peanuts that I had the brilliant idea I mentioned a couple of chapters ago. Rather than blurting it out, however, my native Lancastrian nous (or innate wisdom) made me ponder on my brainwave for a while. As my companions nattered about the shiny black car outside, I focused on the practicalities of my plan and soon concluded that it was such a sure-fire recipe for success that I wished to become one of the cooks.

Noticing my introspective state, Juanjo asked me if they were talking too fast or simply boring me.

"Not at all. The more I think about it, the better the idea sounds to me."

Don Andrés cackled. "Ah, well, I'm not averse to having a partner or two, though I do wish to keep it in the family."

I thought about the money sitting in my new personal account, earning next to no interest, before picturing our house in the village. On the street and around the side there was space for at least three cars, so the expensive step of buying or renting a place to house them could be avoided for the time being, as long as the insurance policy covered vehicles kept out of doors. I knew that restoring vintage cars and selling them at a profit could be a good little earner, so if my scheme failed to take off, we'd be none the worse for it. I suspected that Mónica might not be too keen on the plan, but once I'd explained how foolproof it was, she might come to recognise her partner's astuteness and embrace the idea…

Juanjo chuckled. "Brian's mind has gone into overdrive."

"Steam will soon be coming out of his ears, ha ha."

I pushed back my shoulders and eyed them boldly. "We could rent them out."

"Rent what out?" said Don A.

I smiled. "Ou… your small collection of SEAT motor cars, mainly to holidaymakers, I imagine."

The main man frowned. "Oh, I don't know about that, Brian. I wouldn't want some boy racer behind the wheel of my 1400."

Juanjo tittered. "That's hardly likely. Only enthusiasts and other nostalgic folk would want to rent a car like that. With a Spyder it might be a different story, but then again, youngsters are hardly going to shell out on an 850cc car, however cool it looks."

"The Spyder's engine is 900cc, but I see your point," said Don Andrés. "Well, Brian, I shall mull over your audacious idea, but in principle I'm not convinced."

I shrugged nonchalantly. "I understand that it might… undermine one's sense of ownership. Oh, well, perhaps I'll get hold of a SEAT 600 and see if I have any luck. I believe that folk on holiday would be willing to pay a hundred euros for a fun-packed day for all the family, so it might make me a couple of thousand over the summer, maybe more."

Juanjo pressed his eyes shut, opened them wide, then narrowed the aperture in a manner which seemed to denote a certain degree of cunning. "You'd have to put a limit on the kilometres they can do, just in case someone takes it into their head to shoot off to France for a week."

"That's true, though I expect that most folk will just want to drive along some quiet roads to somewhere nice, maybe with a picnic lunch."

"A hundred kilometres a day, and they'd have to pay extra for any more," Juanjo muttered, before shaking his head rapidly, presumably to clear it of this tempting notion that Cristina might not approve of. I asked him.

"Oh, where cars are concerned, she trusts my judgement, I think."

Don Andrés smiled. "Would you like to come to dinner later, Juanjo? You haven't been for a while."

"Oh, yes, I could do that, thanks."

So we left it at that and soon puttered back to the village.

The conversation I've just reported is as nothing compared to the lengthy debate which took place around the large dining table that evening, so I'll spare you a blow-by-blow account and tell you without too much ado what the upshot was.

Once coffee and infusions had been served, Don Andrés stood up at the head of the table and explained his plan in a very lucid and detailed manner, then handed over to me before the ladies had a chance to pepper him with questions. I'd refined my hypothetical rental scheme by then, and from a seated position I was able to outline a plausible and not overly ambitious scenario in which each of our investments would pay for itself within four or five years, as well as gaining in value during that time. During my speech I kept an eye on Juanjo's reaction and saw that my patter was going down just as well as it used to do with my colleagues at work, most of the time, so I asked him to add his own thoughts to what he'd heard so far.

To my delight he now seemed sold on the scheme and outlined his preferred role in it. He was willing to source and inspect the cars in his spare time, but he'd have to charge almost the going rate for any serious work he did on them, as he couldn't afford to mix his main income stream with a speculative venture. His good friend in Zafra would bring the bodywork up to scratch without charging the earth, so Juanjo hoped to become a regular partner in the enterprise, putting up his share of the money for each car we purchased. He added that he'd be happy to accommodate at least one car on his small forecourt, as the presence of a vintage SEAT would please his customers and might even attract a few new ones.

Don Andrés then invited the ladies to comment and the abovementioned debate began. Lourdes liked the idea in principle, but didn't wish to participate in it, although she believed her daughter Ana might like to get involved in some way, especially after she'd completed her studies. Cristina expressed her concern about spending too much money on such a novel undertaking, but when Juanjo promised to postpone the purchase of his old BMW until success seemed assured, she gave him the green light.

Despite Don Andrés's delight on realising that it seemed likely to become a family affair, Mónica appeared to be our main stumbling block. Buying the vehicles was bound to be a risky business, she said, and our area didn't receive all that many tourists in summer. Holidaymakers were unlikely to wish to travel from the cultural hotspots to Llerena just to go for a drive in an old car, especially if we only had SEATs to offer them.

From the mischievous twinkle in her eyes, I knew she was playing the devil's advocate to some extent, and I believe that her objections helped us to question the wisdom of a plan that had come into being so quickly. When she urged us to sleep on the idea for several nights, we couldn't help but agree that we oughtn't to rush out and buy another

SEAT in the heat of the moment, so we finally broke up in a moderately positive frame of mind.

Before she and I went to sleep, however, she had a good deal more to say on the subject which was for my ears only.

"I'm grateful that you didn't try to exploit my weak spot when you were attempting to convince me," she said as we snuggled up under the thick duvet.

I yawned contentedly. "What's that, love?"

"Our rural lodging, of course."

"Well, it did cross my mind, but I didn't want to complicate matters. If I do manage to convince you, we'll form just a third of the partnership, so our rural lodging didn't seem too relevant."

"It could be for us though. If we can offer vintage car hire as part of our package, it might attract a certain kind of guest who'll then spread the word that we're doing something unique. That's the key, you see, to have something special to offer. I think I'd prefer horse riding myself, but we don't have the knowhow and horses cost a lot to buy and feed, not to mention the land they'd need. Our thing can be old cars, and they'll add spice to the blog I intend to write. An article about a trip somewhere in Papá's lovely old SEAT, with lots of nice photos, will resonate more than yet another typical blog post."

"And in the blog you'll also plug our rural lodging, I assume?"

"Yes, when it's ready. I'd like to take a holistic approach, you see, with one thing… feeding off the other. How does that sound?"

"Wonderful. I'm glad you're feeling more positive at last."

She shrugged. "They say time's a great healer. I'm so glad that Papá has jumped into this car business so quickly. He's wasted no time and it's helping him to get over Mamá's death."

"That's true."

"We should do the same."

"Er, in what way?"

"With the house. Until we finish working on it, it'll scarcely be habitable, so we might as well contract a builder to create our guest accommodation, don't you think?"

I sighed. "You're putting me on the spot, love."

"Ha, and what did you three do to Cristina and me earlier?"

"Hmm, true."

"So what do you say?"

"Let's sleep on it, for several nights."

She giggled. "Fair enough, but not just yet."

So we made love for the first time in ages, and as we lay in each other's arms I felt sure that the die was cast. He who dares wins, as they say, and we were going to give it our best holistic shot.

23

"Take that daft smile off your face, Dad," Ben said three weeks later during our visit to the Jayona iron ore mine, about ten miles to the south of our house which was now in turmoil, as a small team of builders were hacking out the necessary window upstairs, prior to partitioning the rooms and creating our dream holiday let, I hoped. "And try not to look constipated."

I strove to lean more naturally on the wing of the recently polished 1400, before gazing solemnly at the illustrated signboard outside the mine. After prancing around with the camera, taking shots from different angles, Ben asked me to shift and make way for Ana.

"Er, you've taken about a hundred shots of Ana and Mónica today, so if we're to look like a happy family of tourists, I ought to feature too, don't you think?"

"I'll put one of you in the article," said Mónica, by now almost her old self again and busy writing away. With Ben we'd revisited Zafra and Jerez de los Caballeros, and after Ana had arrived from Madrid for a long weekend, we'd checked out the moderately interesting villages of Azuaga and Berlanga, where the 1400 had featured heavily in our photography.

A week or so earlier the Three Motoring Musketeers – as Ben had christened us – had taken possession of a light-blue SEAT 1500, a more angular, American-style car that we'd bought from a private seller in Jaén. Don Andrés, Juanjo and I had made the six-hour round-trip in my Astra, and we believed the rather shabby, spluttering vehicle to be a bargain at €3,700, a price achieved after some theatrical haggling by the main man. After having it trailered home, Juanjo had set about giving the engine a thorough overhaul, prior to handing it over to his bodywork pal who would repair the rusty bits, knock out the dents, and give it a full respray for the modest price of €1000, cash in hand. At present we were appraising the available SEAT 800s – the four-door offspring of the classic 600 – and a well-conserved red one at a garage in Puente Genil, Córdoba was looking like our best bet, though Don Andrés was determined to shave at least a grand off the €7,990 price tag before deigning to drive two hundred kilometres to view it, upon which the old devil intended to haggle some more.

Back to the mine, first exploited in Roman times and situated in a partly man-made ravine in extensive woodland. It had finally closed in 1921, and after decades of abandonment the provincial government had funded a restoration project in the 1990s. The four partly open-air galleries had been made safe and sundry protective barriers installed, before they declared it an official Natural Monument and appointed guides to show visitors around, free of charge, though I believe one has to pay a paltry two euros these days. Our friendly guide, Francisco, described the mine and its flourishing flora and fauna in an entertaining way, but as we followed him around in our yellow helmets I became distracted by Ben's overfriendly manner towards Ana, despite having been told that she had a boyfriend and he was wasting his time.

Being a chip off the old block once removed – my dad was said to have been a bit of a Jack the Lad – Ben had been paying scant heed to this advice, but when I'd rebuked him regarding his wanton desires, he'd insisted that he wasn't trying to seduce her, but to lay the groundwork for a serious romance that might or might not blossom once he'd finished his degree and was free to come to seek his fortune in Spain.

"But she has a long-term boyfriend," I'd said as the two of us strolled around Llerena's main square the previous evening.

"Yeah, well, those long courtships, as you call them, have a habit of fizzling out when a real man comes on the scene. But don't worry, I just aim to make a good impression, then we'll keep in touch and see what develops, if anything. Her mum seems to like me well enough, and that's half the battle, as that lawyer dude sounds like a real stiff."

"A stiff with great earning potential, I believe."

"Yeah, well, now that we're in the classic car trade, I foresee a bright future for myself in Spain."

"I currently have a one-third share in one car," I'd said, as Don Andrés hadn't asked us to buy into the 1400, though he was happy for Mónica and I to rent it out occasionally, as long as we kept it in tiptop shape. "So it's hardly a classic car empire, is it?"

He grinned. "No, but I hope to have other fish to fry as well."

"Like what?"

"You'll see when the time comes," he'd concluded enigmatically.

Anyway, down in the mine I left the flirtatious couple to it, as Ana was old enough to know her own mind, and of course the idea of Ben hooking up with Lourdes's lovely daughter did appeal to me, though I couldn't quite believe that such a fortuitous liaison would come to pass. I began to muse on the SEAT 850 Coupé which we intended to look for once the 800 was in our possession. I'd been wondering if we oughtn't to diversify a bit, because during my online searches I'd come across some apparent bargains, such as a roadworthy, unrusty 1972 Mini for sale in Valladolid for only €4,995. This desire had been vetoed by my partners for the time being, and we soon agreed that four cars would be enough to be going on with.

Initially I'd assumed that we'd set up an official business quite soon, naively believing that we wouldn't have to pay any tax or national insurance until we began to make some money. Don Andrés soon put me straight about this, and even my idea of one of us becoming self-employed and shouldering the responsibility was soon quashed, because in

Spain one has to make substantial monthly payments from the word go, regardless of one's earnings.

That evening at dinner the subject was broached once again and Don Andrés insisted that our cars would have to be hired out in an informal manner for the first year at least, as he'd be damned if he was going to start coughing up before the cash had begun to roll in. To this end the SEAT 1500 had been put in Juanjo's name, while the forthcoming 800 would be mine and the next one Mónica's.

"That way Hacienda (Inland Revenue) won't suspect a thing," he said after sipping the alcohol-free beer which was all he got at home.

"That's all very well, Andrés, but how on earth can we advertise our cars without alerting the taxman to our illegal activity?"

"Oh, on the social media thing that you youngsters use, and in Mónica's travel articles. You'll just have to be careful with the wording."

I scoffed. "How?"

"Oh, you know, by approaching the matter obliquely. You show lots of photos of the cars, and… well, say anything you want without mentioning prices."

"Easier said than done."

"I'll know how to do it," said Mónica. "Besides, it's mainly a question of getting started, then word of mouth should help us to get more customers."

Ana offered to exploit her own social media presence and set up a Facebook page on which she would wax lyrical about the Campiña Sur and insert links to Mónica's blog.

"And I'll do something in England," said Ben, already a favourite of the family and a bosom buddy of Don Andrés, with whom he appeared to have more in common than his own father. "When I come out at Easter we'll make some cool videos with all the cars, then I'll post them on YouTube. Cheer up, Dad. That's the way the world works these days."

"So they say," I muttered, still unconvinced, as I'd seen enough obscure blogs, overlooked Twitter accounts and the like to know that it wasn't so easy to drum up an audience.

"I'll do a little informal networking too," sad Lourdes. "Then, when it's all up and running and you're ready to make it a legitimate business, I'll write an upbeat article and place it in one of the national magazines. How does that sound, Brian?"

"Brilliant." I smiled, then sighed. "But we've an awful long way to go before our enterprise could possibly interest the magazine-reading public. Any serious editor will expect a large array of vintage cars before they'll think it a worthwhile subject to write about."

"Oh, buck up, man," said Don A. "Don't lose sight of the fact that we're doing this mainly for fun. All our cars will be sound investments anyway, so anything we make will be a bonus, but I'm convinced that we *will* make some money. I propose that we use all the means at our disposal, both fair and foul, to target the Easter tourists. If we can rent out the 1400 and the 1500 just once, we'll have made a start and word will spread like wildfire."

"What if someone has an accident?" I whined. "If we make an insurance claim we might end up in hot water with the taxman."

They all regarded me sombrely, except my son, who seemed embarrassed by his father's spinelessness in the face of hypothetical adversity.

"Oh, Dad, don't be such a wet blanket (aguafiestas). If someone crashes, they'll call you. Then you get your skates on and make sure that one of you is holding the keys by the time the pickup truck arrives."

"Hmm, maybe."

After that I ceased to raise further objections and decided to go with the very casual flow which the others seemed to approve of. Later in bed, Mónica subtly pointed out that me having been a company man during my whole working life had made me overcautious about the kind of thing that normal folk took in their stride. She added that if I was going to get stressed about a little thing like hiring out a few old cars, I ought to pull out of the venture and sit back and watch her father and Juanjo make a fortune.

"You've changed your tune," I said in English, as we'd begun to speak it more often so that she wouldn't lose her fluency.

"I didn't have a tune before, but now I foresee a gentle, melodious one with a few bits of staccato now and then, just to spice things up. Try to think of all this – the cars, the lodging, the blog, and whatever else we may do – as an adventure, but the mild adventure of two middle-aged people who don't *need* to do any of it if we don't wish to. If our plans fail we can go on with our walking, socialising and pottering around, just like everyone else does."

"That sounds sort of boring, now you come to mention it."

"Of course it does. Now, go to sleep and begin tomorrow in a more carefree frame of mind, please."

"I'll try."

***

Mónica's little pep talk seemed to do the trick and I did cease to fret quite so much about things which were mostly outside my control anyway. At the end of the day, we'd each be responsible for the vehicle we actually owned, so when *my* red SEAT 800 arrived towards the end of March – having cost €7,250 in the end – I soon became immensely proud of the tidy little car which we began to use more often than the Astra.

By then the builders had almost finished the apartment and we'd reformed enough of the main house to satisfy us for the time being, so we hoped to move in before Ben's arrival at Easter. We agreed that it would be better for him not to sleep under the same roof as Ana, as although her stiff of a boyfriend had yet to be sacked, she and Ben had been speaking regularly. It looked like the writing was on the wall for the trainee lawyer, but we wanted Ana to do the right thing by him, rather than be lured into bed by my shameless son.

Juanjo was about to inspect a light-blue SEAT 850 saloon in Badajoz, priced at only €6000 despite its purportedly excellent condition, possibly because over half a million of them had been produced, the last in 1974, so it wasn't quite as sought after as its three stablemates. This was to be our last purchase of the year, we promised ourselves, because if our rental scheme did fail to prosper, we'd have to think long and hard about our next move. So far our collective efforts on social media hadn't met with much success, though a friend of a friend of Juanjo and Cristina was going to hire the 1400 for a few days over Easter, to visit some relatives in Plasencia. This entailed a 500km round trip which our chief mechanic felt confident that the sturdy car would manage without a hitch, though he intended to place several large bottles of water and a can of oil in the boot, just in case.

Don Andrés was loving every minute of our efforts to get our motorised show on the road, and one morning in our favourite bar in Villagarcía de la Torre he confided that the whole thing had given him a new lease of life. Although he still missed his wife terribly, their relationship had deteriorated in recent years to a point where their initially blithesome squabbling had become an ongoing battle between two people of very different temperaments. This had caused him to let himself go and come close to being carried off by La Parca (the Grim Reaper), or so he claimed, but now he had every intention of living to a hundred.

Lourdes had settled into the household, and since we'd soon be leaving it, she intended to stay on in the big old place to keep her father company. Ana would join her there in July – when she wasn't in Cáceres with her much-maligned dad – before entering the world of work, one way or another, although like Ben she didn't aspire to become a lifelong employee as I'd been. Not that I regretted that too much at the time, because I was happier than I'd ever been and looked forward to a long and hopefully healthy life with Mónica, and her family, of course.

If there's an air of finality about this chapter, it's because a whole new chapter in our lives was about to commence which will be the subject of a second book, so it's now time for me to draw a line under my formative months in Extremadura and recharge my writing batteries before tackling the eventful summer which lay ahead of us.

As Mónica said in our main upstairs bedroom while we were making up our new king-sized bed: "One must do everything with enthusiasm, but always know when to draw the line."

So I'll take her advice and sign off for now. Thank you for following our story so far, and I hope to offer you the next instalment before the end of 2023.

Written somewhere in the Campiña Sur, Extremadura,
February to November, 2022.
Brian J. Wilson

Printed in Great Britain
by Amazon